CUBAN LEGENDS

Illustrations by
Siegfried Kaden

 Markus Wiener
Publishers

PRINCETON

 Ian Randle
Publishers

KINGSTON

CUBAN LEGENDS

Selected and Introduced by
Salvador Bueno

Translated from Spanish by
Christine Ayorinde

For information write to:
Markus Wiener Publishers, 231 Nassau Street, Princeton, NJ 08542

Book design by Cheryl Mirkin

Library of Congress Cataloging-in-Publication Data

Leyendas cubanas. English
    Cuban Legends/selected and introduced by Salvador Bueno;
        translated from Spanish by Christine Ayorinde;
        illustrated by Siegfried Kaden.
    Includes bibliographical references.
    ISBN 1-55876-284-1 (hc)
    ISBN 1-55876-285-x (pbk)
    1. Legends—Cuba.
    I. Bueno, Salvador.   II. Title.
    GR121.C8. L4913 2002
    398.2'097291—dc21   2002016726

First published in Jamaica 2003 by
Ian Randle Publishers, 11 Cunningham Avenue, Box 686, Kingston 6
    ISBN 976-637-071-0 paperback
    A catalogue record for this book is available from the
    National Library of Jamaica.

Printed in the United States of America on acid-free paper.

Table of Contents

PART THREE • 159

Foreword

When we use the word "legend" in conversation there is a chance our interlocutors may not know exactly what it is we are referring to. They will need to pay more attention to the context than to the word itself because the term can mean many different things. For this reason, it is essential to start with a definition before going on to look in greater detail at the theme of this work: Cuban legends. Legends are studied across many different disciplines and therefore we must decide what constitutes a legend and set its boundaries so it does not become confused with other types of story.

The etymology of "legend" derives from the Latin *legere*. In the 1970 edition of the dictionary of the Real Academia Española de la Lengua (Royal Academy of the Spanish Language), the first definition is: "the action of reading"; the second: "a work that is read"; the third: "a story or collection of saints' lives"; and the fourth: "an account of happenings that are more imaginary than real." If we set aside the definitions of this hefty tome, we may recall that, for many centuries, the term "legend" referred primarily to the "lives of the saints." This was on account of *The Golden Legend*, a work written in the thirteenth century by Jacopo de Varazze, more commonly known as Jacobus de Voragine, which became a best-seller. However, this information does not resolve our attempts at finding a definition.

Because of its literary qualities, the term seems to have a wider application. We should therefore turn to a specialist dictionary, for example, the *Dictionary of World Literature* by Joseph T. Shirley.[1] This informs us that the legend is "a fictitious narrative, embellished with popular historical material, which people sometimes believe to be historical." This definition comes very close to the fourth meaning offered by the *Diccionario de la Real Academia*. With this information, we can now attempt to define more precisely the parameters of these narratives, tales, or stories.

Every people preserves a wealth of legends that are handed down orally through the generations. These narratives, traditional or fictitious, belong to what is loosely termed "the folkloric tale." According to anthropologists who specialize in this area, this comprises three narrative forms: "tale," "myth," and "legend." The anthropologist William Bascom, cited by Susana Chertudi in her book, *El cuento folklórico* (The Folkloric Tale)[2] states that: "tales are prose narratives considered to be fictitious," in which the action takes place anytime and anywhere and whose characters may be human or nonhuman. Myths are narrations that, "in the society where they are recounted are considered to be real events that took place in the remote past." They are usually sacred and are linked to ritual and dogma. The action takes place in a different world, and the main characters are not human. Legends, like rituals, "are believed to be true stories by narrator and listeners, but they are located in a time seen as less remote, when the world was like it is today. We would add that elements which locate them in time and space are common in legends."

One should bear in mind that some traditional tales are typically used to explain the origins of or reason behind something. In this case they are termed etiological. When they deal with the development of accidents or phenomena of nature: animals, plants, man, and his institutions, place names, and so on, they are also termed explanatory. However, depending on the content or characteristics, and also the cultural context in which they are produced, such tales or narratives can be either myths or legends. To sum up, while it is the product of a distant collective memory, what distinguishes the legend from the myth is the fact that it contains more elements of historical veracity. It takes place in familiar times and places. These are specified by those who hand down these stories, though such details will often vary between the different versions collected by researchers.

But one should not imagine that these legends only originated in times long past. According to A. van Gennep in his book *La forma-ción de las leyendas* (The Formation of Legends)[3]: "the formation of legends is not a thing of the past; they are appearing all the time." Over the last few centuries and on every continent, legends have appeared. They are spread or circulated orally and are nearly always sustained by superstition and ignorance. Magical or fantastic tales, rooted in reality to give them greater authenticity and greater reso-nance, are transmitted in this manner, by word of mouth, down the generations. A combination of fantasy and ignorance sustains these stories. Legends or myths are used to explain events that, for simple minds, do not have an obvious, rational explanation. Karl Marx right-ly noted that "Mythology subdues, dominates and moulds the forces of nature and it disappears when these forces have truly been domi-nated."

For many years, confusion reigned among scholars as to the dif-ference between myths, legends, and folkloric tales. This is why dif-ferent types of narrative are found jumbled together in a number of works. The compilers have not taken the trouble to decide which cat-egory the tales included in their volumes should fall into. Paulo de Carvalho-Neto in his *History of Ibero-American Folklore*[4] attempts to define the overlapping boundaries between myths and legends. This also needs to be done for legends and traditions. According to the Brazilian anthropologist, "the legend is an imaginary narrative that contains elements of truth and which is also linked to a particular region. It deals with heroic themes, the history of the nation, mytho-logical creatures, spirits, saints, or it explains the origins of various events. The myth is almost always a product of fear though, strictly speaking, the legends that originated as the result of fear are the mythological and animistic ones only." For Carvalho-Neto, legends can be: heroic, historical, mythological, animistic, religious, or etio-logical.

The enormous stock of traditional legends that are studied by

anthropologists is thrown out of focus when a new element—the literary—is introduced. Ever since the pre-Romantic and Romantic
writers began to turn their attention to the popular narratives and legends of their countries, a new literary category emerged that some
called legend and others tradition. In 1697 Perrault published his
Histories or tales of past times. At the height of the Romantic era, the
Brothers Grimm achieved fame in German literature with the tales
they collected in 1810 from peasants in Hesse. In 1820, Walter Scott
carried out a similar undertaking in English. What the French call
popular traditions were more precisely termed folklore, coined from
folk and lore "knowledge" in 1846 by W. J. Thomas. This prepared
the way for a new discipline called "folk wisdom" or "folklore." It
includes not just traditional tales but also studies of popular culinary
traditions, folk medicine and dances, music, instruments, costume,
adornment, masks, songs, and proverbs.

In the latter half of the last century it became fashionable for
Spanish American writers to invent literary traditions like those of
Ricardo Palma in his book, *Peruvian Traditions*. These "traditions"
are not easy to define. Another famous Peruvian, Manuel Gutiérrez
Prada, described those written by his compatriot as: "a bittersweet
misrepresentation of history." Without wishing to query the aptness of
this definition, we should bear in mind that Palma unfolded the entire
course of Peruvian history in his traditions: anecdotes, gossip,
rumors, stock phrases, and proverbs. He made use of everything, but
the main focus was always the history of his country before and after
the arrival of the Spanish conquistadors, from the Viceroyalty up until
the Republic. Throughout Spanish America, "traditionists" began to
emerge, to greater or lesser literary acclaim, but none had the wit and
guile of Palma. The legend should not be confused with the tradition.
The latter rests on historical fact, however scanty, even though it is
fictionalized and disguised and always specifies (if vaguely) dates
and times. Nevertheless, in many Latin American countries, legends

and traditions are lumped together in works edited by compilers from very different disciplines.

In the case of Cuban legends, our people has an extremely varied repertoire originating from the cultures that mixed together on our soil. Fernando Ortiz rightly said that Cuba was an "ajiaco," that is, a melting-pot in which different peoples and cultures fused to create what he termed "transculturation." This neologism he coined perfectly describes the mutual integration, the process of give and take, and the interpenetration of two or more cultures. From this dialectical process a synthesis is produced, in this case, Cuban culture, mestizo culture, mulatto culture.

The extensive cultural mixing in Cuba is the result of the various origins of those who settled here long before the European discovery of America. In ancient times, the verdant territory of Cuba was a place where migrants from the cold north met those who came from the hot islands of the Lesser Antilles. Since then, Cuba has been place of transit, "the crossroads of the world" as its exemplary son José Martí described it. Along with the Spaniards from quite different regions of Spain (Castilians, Andalusians, Extremadurans, etc.), came Portuguese, Levantines, and Italians. They were soon followed by people with a somewhat darker complexion who suffered the ignominy and humiliation of slavery. First they were brought from Hispaniola and Spain, and later directly from Africa. They were brutally snatched from various parts of that continent, mainly from its Atlantic coasts, Guinea, Congo, and Angola, but also from the more distant coasts on the other side, the ports of Zanzibar and Mozambique on the Indian Ocean.

All of these people, along with others who arrived from Macao and Canton in Asia as well as Europeans from different nations, brought with them their beliefs and superstitions, their myths and legends. In Cuba these cultural elements combined to produce the singularly mixed character of our national culture. This is why, among the leg-

ends that have been collected in our country, we find those that have
their origin in the Pre-Colombian indigenous culture, those that
derive from the various African cultural strands and those that are of
Spanish extraction and were transplanted in this Antillean isle.

Many of the legends with indigenous themes appear to be somewhat loose and idealized reconstructions by writers who were enthu-
siastic about our Taino or Siboney past. It is true that the European
conquest led to the extinction of the indigenous population. However,
it must be pointed out that, despite this rapid disappearance in over
less than a century, many place names and geographical features in
our country still bear their original Indian names. Among the traces
of indigenous cultures is, for example, the bohío,[5] now fast disappearing from the Cuban landscape thanks to the transformations of
the socialist Revolution. Nevertheless, the authenticity of many of the
apparently indigenous legends is extremely dubious. The early chron-
iclers of the Conquest of the Antilles collected little material of this
kind from Indian informants. That is why one may question the
authenticity of many of the legends that are absolutely riddled with
indigenous names. They were part of the mid-nineteenth-century
Siboneyist movement introduced to our literature by José Fornaria,
Joaquín Lorenzo Luaces, and Juan Cristóbal Nápoles Fajardo, El
Cucalambé. The so-called Indian legends reveal the fictitious and ide-
alistic quality of these pseudo-indigenous poems.

With the legends of African origin it is quite the opposite. They
were generally collected in the twentieth century by researchers with
an academic agenda. During the colonial era, the prevailing caste system of the slave society considered barbaric and primitive everything
that originated from those human beings, whom the dominant classes of the period, the slave traders and sugarmill owners considered
simply "pieces of coal," merchandise, mere things according to
Roman law, as a character in Cirilo Villaverde's novel *Cecilia Valdés*
recalls. However, despite the cultural compartmentalization of the

colonial period, transculturation inevitably took place, as some intellectuals of Domingo del Monte's circle had already pointed out in the mid-nineteenth century.

During the 1868 War of Independence, which initiated a century of struggle, Cuban nationality began to be consolidated and defined through the national integration of blacks, mulattos, and whites who bravely challenged the might of Spanish colonialism. The Cuban patriots believed that they could not gain independence for their native land if they did not also grant freedom to the thousands of slaves suffering under that system of dispossession. Slavery was ended by those who were fighting for independence, and between 1880 and 1886, the Spanish metropolitan government was compelled to decree its abolition.

But the North American intervention in the battle between the Cubans and the colonial government, and the subsequent establishment of the neocolonial and annexed Republic, allowed racial discrimination to continue and with it the exclusion and oppression of the black and mulatto population and their cultural manifestations. The campaign initiated by the anthropologist, sociologist, and folklorist Fernando Ortiz (1881–1969), aimed both to study the elements of African cultures transplanted in our country and to eliminate the racial discrimination that persisted in Cuban society. Following his early books on this subject, *Los negros brujos* (The Black Witchdoctors) (1906) and *Los negros esclavos* (The Black Slaves) (1917), Ortiz founded the Archivos del folklore cubano in 1924 and in 1938 the journal *Estudios afrocubanos*. Both publications contained numerous examples of folkloric expressions of African origin including traditions, legends, myths, and so on. The researcher Rómulo Lachatañeré collaborated in this undertaking. In 1938 he published *Oh, mío Yemayá*. Lydia Cabrera brought out *Cuentos negros de Cuba* in 1940. The poet and folklorist Ramón Guirao published *Órbita de la poesía afrocubana* (1938), which included folkloric material and later, *Cuentos y leyendas afrocubanas* (1942). The interest aroused by the studies of Fernando Ortiz stimulated the vast output of artistic and literary works on this theme from 1928 onward in Cuba. Among them were the poems "Rumba Dancer" by Ramón Guirao and "The Rumba" by José Tallet, as well as pieces of classical music inspired by African rhythms composed by Alejandro García Caturla and Amadeo Roldán. The trend culminated in the work of Nicolás Guillén.

In the various districts, regions, and towns of Cuba, legends and traditions that originated after the Spanish Conquest and colony can be found. Some betray their Spanish origin; others are Creole. A great many are what the experts call "etiological," and they are embellished by the popular imagination. Other legends are linked to the heroic struggles of the Cuban people. These began to circulate at the beginning of the Wars of Independence. As early as the first decades of the twentieth century, during the annexed and neocolonial Republic, some authors who were interested in traditions and legends began to collect them as testimony to their love for their native city or region. We must remember the work of Manuel García Garófalo Mesa, Adrián del Valle, and others. The collection of folkloric pieces published by the Central University of Las Villas is extremely important, as are the determined efforts of Samuel Feijóo in this field. These are continued competently in the journal *Signos*, produced by the National Council for Culture, which is also edited by the multifaceted Feijóo.

Nor should the aforementioned literary legends be left out of a collection like this one. The legend entitled "The White Vulture," by Gertrudis Gómez de Avellaneda, is very famous in the Hispanic world of letters. It is inspired by one of the many legends of her native Camagüey. Another legend, "The Light of Yara," by the costumbrista and patriot Luis Victoriano Betancourt, is linked to the independence struggles of the Cuban people. In it the indigenous past is intertwined with the struggle that was taking place at the time when the author from Havana was writing it.

Some may perhaps wish to question the value or otherwise of this retelling of Cuban legends. Objections and doubts have sometimes been raised about the dissemination of the more fantastic and incredible popular tales that include both fairy tales and legends. The great Maxim Gorky, who had enormous respect for anything that came out of the creative genius of the common people, wrote of "the wonderful capacity of our minds to see beyond facts." And the most fantastic examples he recalled were the "flying carpets," which, centuries ago, enabled the popular imagination to anticipate the invention of the airplanes and even spaceships of today. Legends, like traditional stories for children, serve to stimulate the imagination and may even inculcate positive values. Legends, their qualities and limitations notwithstanding, nonetheless inspire the imagination, and it is only as a product of the imagination that they should be assessed.

This book is not intended to be an exhaustive selection of Cuban legends. It is simply a compilation or sample of the vast panorama of tales of a legendary nature from the various areas and regions of our country. The primary consideration was not the literary merit of these narratives, some of which are traditions rather than genuine legends, but their representative value. Vestiges of the superstition and ignorance that reigned during the Spanish colony and into the neocolonial Republic, they give us a flavor of times past. But they also offer us examples of resistance and the love of freedom. In fact, the subject matter of the legends could be rewritten from a contemporary point of view to incorporate the ideological stances that are the basis of our socialist Revolution. This compilation may, perhaps, serve as an incentive for such an undertaking.

Salvador Bueno

Part One

Caucubú

Caucubú[1] was the most beautiful woman in the chiefdom of Guamuhaya. She was the daughter of Chief Manatiguahuraguana, who ruled over the district where the village of Mancanilla, now Trinidad de Cuba, was situated. The Indians used to play their bato games on the outskirts of the village buildings. At night burning guava logs perfumed the air and illuminated the curvaceous hips of the women who danced the areíto.[2] Their bodies, made firm by the physical nature of their labors appeared rosy and lustrous in the light. Its reflection on the precious stones of their loincloths and on the sheen of their black hair was dazzling. Then Caucubú would be taken from the hut built by her father the chief and placed under a canopy of palm leaves decorated with lilies, shells from the near-by beaches carpeting the ground, in a prominent position for the performance.

She was declared the queen of the feast, and all the young Indians burned with passion for the charming girl. Her beauty and goodness enchanted her noble father, who dreamed for her of an empire or wealth greater than what he possessed.

From Ornofay, Magón, Escambray, Sabana, Sabaneque, Jagua, and even from distant Camagüey, the first-born sons of chiefs came at different times to ask for her hand in marriage. But it was in vain. Caucubú was affectionate and attentive to all without accepting the love of any. She handed out smiles as sweet as pineapples and as pure as the essence of flowers. She sent her suitors' mothers and sisters fine hammocks woven by her lovely hands and items of adornment made from the gold collected by her father on his excursions to the gold-bearing lands of Mabujina or Arimao.

Poor Caucubú! Those who did not know her true feelings used to say that she lived without love. But Caucubú loved and was loved in return but had to pretend that she did not wish to marry. She concealed her love from her father's eyes so that he would not force her to accept one of her suitors.

The man chosen by her heart was Naridó,[3] a young Indian who lived on the other side of the Guanayara. There he devoted himself to hunting and fishing, pastimes at which he excelled and that ensured his and his family's upkeep. But his entire soul was devoted to the object of his love, his sweet Caucubú, the most beautiful and the noblest woman in the chiefdom of Guamuhaya, who remained true to the love of the poor Indian.

The good lovers had already suffered several setbacks. On one occasion, when Naridó was fishing at the mouth of the Guanayara, he was caught in a hurricane and his canoe was tossed beyond Cabagán. Caucubú, whose compassion was known to her father, persuaded him to send his servants to look for the shipwrecked man, and he was saved miraculously.

Another time it was Naridó who was on the verge of dying of a broken heart believing he had lost forever the object of his love. The chief had decided to send Caucubú to the court of Chief Guacanayabo. Everything was ready for the departure. The lightest canoes of the region navigated the rivers and coasts. They met at the calm mouth of the Guaurabo to escort the beautiful daughter of the powerful master to the dominion of Guacabino,[4] the young chief of that province. He was brave and stronger than most. On more than one occasion he had defeated the Caribs from the other Antilles who dared invade their coasts.

Fortunately for Caucubú and Naridó, a courier arrived on the day before the flotilla was due to depart with Caucubú, who perhaps would be declared the wife of the fierce Indian from Guacanayabo. He announced that the Caribs were planning a large expedition to the coasts of Cuba. It was feared they were coming to take revenge on Guacabino, the chief of Guacanayabo.

Caucubú's father called off the journey so as not to risk his daughter's being captured by the invaders. He acted wisely for, some time later, it was discovered that the Carib expedition had defeated Guacabino's forces, and he died in the fighting. Guacabino was one of the most powerful chiefs. Had he been captivated by her beauty, Caucubú's father would not have refused him her hand.

But these setbacks were nothing compared to the troubles the two lovers suffered as the result of the ambitions of the Indian women, mainly the wives of the other chiefs, who wished to see the Chief Manatiguahuraguana's daughter married to one of their sons.

Poor people in that part of the world also suffered the tortures of love and lovesick hearts had to overcome a thousand obstacles to attain the happiness they dreamed of. And why not? After all, they were human beings subject to all passions.

Caucubú and Naridó, the exemplary lovers, were envied. Inevitably they were hounded by terrible enemies who were jealous of the happiness that would be theirs on the day the powerful chief of Guamuhaya, a father first but also a ruler, would make her happy by uniting her with the man her heart had chosen.

For the time being, in his travels along the Guaurabo, poor Naridó admired in the stars the loving eyes of the beautiful Caucubú and in the river's reeds, the supple waist of the adorable girl. In the warbling of the mockingbird he heard the sweet voice that had sworn to love him despite all the obstacles. In the flowers that grew by the river of their homeland, he saw the ornaments with which he would one day crown the thick black hair of the maiden he desired.

The arrival of the whites disturbed the rhythm of the agreeable life of the Taínos of the region. One fine day the Indians were gazing at what, for them, was the strange sight of Columbus's arrival. He was obliged to spend the night with his ships lying off the coast of Guamuhaya's kingdom. It is said that from his ship the great admiral could hear the noise of the Indians at their areítos and smell the unmistakable aroma of the smoke from the burning guava branches and tobacco leaves.

Later Ojeda arrived. He was traveling through the region carrying among his possessions the most prized relic—a statue of the Virgin believed to be the one later found floating on the waters of the bay of Nipe, which would be identified as the statue of the Virgin of Charity of El Cobre.

Then Diego Velázquez arrived, en route for Jagua. Manatiguahuraguana, along with all the great men of the district, offered him feasts so sumptuous that the famous colonizer changed his plans. Instead of proceeding to Jagua for Christmas, he decided to stay in Mancanilla and await the results of the expedition led by Narváez and Father de las Casas, who had been sent to the western part of the island. During the feasts the Spaniards noticed Caucubú's in-

comparable beauty. Her eyes caught the attention of the conquistadors. From then on word of her beauty began to spread throughout Cuba. However, no one could fathom the secret of the tender
and kind but also penetrating and steady gaze that was typical of
the incomparable countenance of that lovely girl.

The town of Trinidad was founded. As it grew, new colonizers
arrived. With each group came fresh suitors who vainly attempted
to win Caucubú's love. The demands of love became a veritable
onslaught, and persecution and ill-treatment were the order of the
day.

The indigenous people no longer spoke in simple, innocent, and
sincere words. Their demeanor, according to Las Casas, the sweetest and gentlest in the world, became one of utter silence. Caucubú
also lost her sweet smile. The expression on her face changed into
one of constant, quiet seriousness that enhanced the subdued
majesty of her beauty.

Naridó could no longer hunt. He belonged to one of Father de
las Casas's encomiendas.[5] He toiled miserably and felt intense
hatred. His love seemed ever more impossible. His hatred of
whites was not due to the work he did—his master was one of the
better ones. He hated them because they were breaking his heart
by trying to remove his one great love from his life. Caucubú, seeing her father's misery at the abuse and the loss of his chiefdom,
did not wish to add to his sorrow and was afraid to confess the
whole truth to him.

Days went by, maybe months. Things continued to get worse.
One day, Porcayo de Figueroa arrived in town. He had a reputation
for brutality and cruelty. As he was passing through, carried by
Indians in his sedan chair, he managed to look on the beauty of
Caucubú, who sat under a leafy carob tree gazing in a distracted

manner at the landscape of the lovely valley. Her gaze held the frustrated recollection of her life, as if she wished to see in it her beloved Naridó or her former subjects who adored her. Vasco Porcayo, who was dictatorial, brutish, and overbearing, wanted Caucubú for himself. But she rebelled and, availing herself of her agility, strength, and youth, managed to escape his murderous henchmen. Running swiftly, she crossed the Vicunia valley. Eluding Porcayo's guard, she entered the darkness of the Magic Cave, which became her place of captivity, the cell of her sentiments, the prison where she would end her days.

Naridó, despairing when he heard of the events from his companions, wept with rage and revealed his great love to Father de las Casas. He told him what had happened, of Porcayo's fury at the defiance of an Indian girl whom he was not able to find, and of the extremes resorted to by the soldiers when confronted with failure. All the searches they ordered proved fruitless. They even captured and killed her father, who was happy to accept death to escape from such injustice. Naridó, made desperate by such abuse, attempted to attack Porcayo with his stone axe, but one blow of a young soldier's saber put an end to his young life. Father de las Casas managed to have the bodies of Caucubú's father and lover laid to rest side by side. The group of Indians were filled with sorrow. Grief etched itself on their faces in condemnation of such a savage deed. Father de las Casas felt compelled to abandon all the encomiendas and goods he had been granted. Thereafter he devoted his life to pleading with the world for the freedom to this noble indigenous race.

The tradition tells how at night, the Indians took Caucubú their choicest fruit and left the most beautiful flowers at the entrance of the Magic Cave, a custom that was continued until the death of the last Taíno in our region. They say that, on moonlit nights when the north winds whisper in the trees on the hill near the entrance to the cave, Caucubú appears in all her beauty, the loveliest woman of the chiefdom of Guamuhaya.

The Legend of Canímar (1)

In the western region of the island lived the great Chief Baguanao in the prosperous settlement of Yucayo that stood on the shores of the bay of the same name. Three great rivers flowed into it: the Babonao, the Guainey, and the Jibacabuya, and the little River Güeybaque (today called the Buey-Vaca). Chief Baguanao was unhappy. It was not long since his son Caburni had died. Now he had only the mischievous Yumuri, who was ten, and the beautiful Cibayara, who was fifteen. Worse still, his wife, Acanaguaya, was unable to forget her son, Caburni, the best warrior and fisherman in Yucayo. But the sea had been envious of the sixteen-year-old Caburni, who seemed older because of his skill as a warrior and fisherman. It had made him fall into its watery embrace and hid him forever.

Acanaguaya was grinding corn with her daughter Cibayara. They were talking of the visit of Camují, the famous warrior from the Babonao valley and adviser to Chief Guaneney. The behíque[6] Macaorí had cured Camují of the fevers that can kill. They had heard this from Baguanao after Camují had gone away. And they also knew that the behíque Macaorí had ordered Camují to hand over to the Bat God all his fine axes, daggers, his favorite spear, decorated pots, and even the dujo[7] or ornamental stool that Chief Guaneney had presented to him, contrary to custom. To the amazement of all, as only chiefs use dujos, he kept it in his bohío.

In order to deliver these riches to the Bat God, Camují went into the middle of the River Jibacabuya and threw everything into the water. As Macaorí the behíque had explained, that river is the place where offerings to the god are left.

From the heights of Guarabaibo (known today as la Cumbre), Canimao looked down on his village. Yucayo stood at the mouth of the Guainey (where the Vigia Place with the Sauto Theater and the law courts, and so on, now stand), and his eyes searched for the bohío of his beloved Cibayara. Then he looked farther into the distance toward the heights of Dabonico (now called Monserrate). He then turned back toward Yucayo, where he knew that Cibayara would be waiting for him.

And Canimao was happy. He had hunted three large jutías.[8] He decided to take two as a gift for Chief Baguanao and present the other to his beloved mother, the widowed Manaobara. Manaobara handed her son a shell cup filled with delicious telenque (wild rosemary boiled to produce a drink like tea or coffee). His mother gazed at him lovingly while Canimao slowly savored the telenque. He was thinking that when he married Cibayara she would be the one to give him the delicious telenque.

No one knew how it came to pass, but Cibayara stayed in her hammock for three days. Her flesh burned, and her whole body was consumed with the fever that kills. No one knew how to cure her. Baguanao was stony-faced with despair, and Acanaguaya silently feared that the gods wanted to take her daughter to where her departed son was. After speaking to her husband, Acanaguaya sent little Yumurí to go and look for Canimao. Perhaps the behíque

Macaorí would be able to cure Cibayara just as he had cured Camují's fever. When Canimao arrived, Chief Baguanao told him to go to the bank of the river Jibacabuya where Macaori lived and to bring him back. He ordered him to take the twenty-man canoe so that he would reach there quickly.

To Canimao's surprise, Macaorí was waiting for him. There at the top of a hill overlooking the River Jibacabuya was Macaorí's bohío. He stood in the doorway. Canimao's companions stayed beside the canoe. Canimao was alone with the behíque. He knew then that his beloved Cibayara would be saved and that she would be his wife. But he would have to repay the Bat God for this. Canimao swore before the god's clay image that he would give him whatever he asked in exchange for Cibayara's life and health.

Cibayara began to laugh again. Once more she became a flower in Canimao's eyes. The Bat God had ordered Macaorí to cure Cibayara for, as he announced to the great Chief Baguanao, she would give birth to a man who would make a woman who killed for love sleep like a stone. That woman was already being carried in the womb of someone's wife. Macaorí said no more and left. Acanaguaya's maternal heart was like a kiss on the feet of the Bat God.

Canimao and his wife, Cibayara, were happy. The bohío that rose among the branches that overhung the waters of the River Guainey was the peaceful setting for their love. Cibayara had held inside her for three months the seed of a male child planted by Canimao's love. Canimao said: "It will be a boy; the behíque has already prophesied it. A son who will honor us." And the couple dreamed, wrapped in their love.

Alone in his canoe, Canimao returned to where the behíque Macaorí had to repay the Bat God for Cibayara's life. He had known since before the wedding that he would have to pay a high price. Knowing it, he left his house as soon as night fell, taking advantage of Cibayara's sleep so as not to have to say good-bye to her. The moon was rising, rising. It was already so high that it cast its silvery hue, like flashing scales, on the River Jibacabuya a. A small canoe reached the middle of the river. Canimao stood alone in it. Slowly he lifted the hand holding a dagger and uncovering his chest to death, fell into the river.

Cibayara gave birth to her son. Every full moon she took offerings to the River Jibacabuya, which she and everyone else now called river of Canimao. And due to the colonizers' mishearing, the River Canimao became the River Canímar that we all know, and the little River Güeybaque became the Buey Vaca of today.

The Light of Yara

It was a terrible and somber night. The ominous wings of the black bird of the Conquest began to overshadow the beautiful skies of Cuba. The land of America, once virgin and pure, trampled now by alien feet, was saturated with the blood spilled by the tyrannical invader. The rivers flowed lugubrious and melancholy, their currents swollen with the tears of the newly enslaved. The tropical breezes fled in consternation to hide their sorrow in the remotest jungles of the American realm.

It was the agony of the freed slave. A huge bonfire rose, terrible and menacing, in the middle of the vast plain of Yara. A hundred fiendish monsters danced frenziedly round it. A young Indian stood beside it, fearlessly and calmly awaiting the signal for the sacrifice. He listened intently to the words of comfort and resignation offered for his soul by an old priest who urged him to convert to Christianity in return for eternal life in Heaven. "Is Heaven very beautiful?" asked the Indian with simple candor.

"Very beautiful," the old man answered, "very beautiful, for that is where God is."

"And do Spaniards also go to Heaven?" asked the Indian.

"Yes," answered the old man, "those who are good."

"Well in that case," interrupted the Indian, "I don't want to go to Heaven because I don't want to live with them even in Heaven."

Those monsters were the conquistadors; that old man was Friar Bartolomé de las Casas, and that Indian was Hatuey.

At last the signal for the sacrifice was given. Hatuey threw himself bravely into the all-consuming flames. The Spaniards let out savage howls of joy, and Bartolomé de las Casas fell to his knees, sending up a funeral prayer to Heaven as the Angel of Liberty gathered up in her wings the last breath of the first martyr of Cuban independence.

Ever since then the dim and mysterious light of the huge bonfire roams around those wide plains by night, keeping watch over those who still sleep in dismal bondage, awaiting the hour of eternal enlightenment and of eternal vengeance. That light was the spirit of Hatuey. It was the light of Yara.

Three centuries passed. One night the roving light stopped at the same spot where Hatuey's bonfire had been built. And at that moment, the palm trees of Cuba, those silent specters of the Indians, shook their extravagant plumes violently, and the heavens lit up with a pure and brilliant clarity. The innermost depths of the earth trembled. Kindled by the wild storm, the dim and mysterious light became a huge flame that spread rapidly with the wind to rouse all hearts, purify all souls, and sanctify all freedoms. It was the light of Yara, come to take its revenge. It was the tomb of Hatuey that now became the cradle of Independence. It was the tenth of October.

The Funeral

On the beaches of Guaicanamá stood neat ecraras,[9] which from a distance, out at sea, looked as if they were floating on the waves. The beaches of the peaceful settlement of humble and brave fisherfolk appeared to be on fire. Many groups of people carrying flaming torches traversed the sand in a boisterous crowd. The fires cast their reflection on the huts by the shore and spread patterned squiggles that looked like gold moiré ribbons on the surface of the water.

From a distance, the to-ing and fro-ing of the lights, made hazy by the clouds of smoke, resembled the outlandish race of the Romans. It was a fishing party. Nibo the Nitaíno had invited his followers. Among those present was Caonareyto,[10] the prolific balladeer of the region. Accompanied by the maguei,[11] and the lambí,[12] he sang in flowing verse of the tradition of his forefathers, the chief's exploits, the manly tribulations of the hunt, and the sweet prospect of their loves. At the party were other personages from Guanabacoa and even from Mayanabo, and most important of all, the adored Bayacú. Everything was ready: light and solidly built mahogany canoes packed with fire-hardened wooden fish spears, agave nets, bone fish hooks, cassava, banana tree, and tobacco. The servants waited, resting upright on the paddles, and the musicians, with their bulging cheeks and restless hands, were eager to play their whistles and the small drum.

The dance began, and lads and maidens holding hands spun in wide circles around Caonareyto, the rustic master of ceremonies of the cotillion. They invoked Nonum,[13] and as the Boitio[14] declared that she was smiling on them, he gave them the order to depart. From the darkest corner of the bay in the little inlet of Guanabacoa came frightened shouting. In the light of the torches that swiftly rushed to the spot, Nibo could be seen tearing his hair as he protested to heaven, crying in anguish: "Atabeira,[15] give me my daughter!"

Bayacú's body did not appear. An escaping cajaya fish had overturned her canoe, and the girl remained underneath. On the beaches of Guaicanamá with their neat ecraras, by light of the spluttering torches, working together in silence, the guests trampled the sand as they walked slowly to and fro. Neither the people in the packed canoes nor the waiting flutists, heads bowed in silent grief and fear, dared look at the couch of royal palm surrounded by leaves and feathers. There Bayacú lay, and squatting at her side, her father, the chief. The dead girl lay there, her mouth half open, not a blemish on her skin, as if the spirit of the sea had not wished to spoil her beauty. Imagine her smiling, shrouded in her black and abundant hair, here and there faint traces of rouge, jagua,[16] and indigo that looked like congested blood on the surface of her body. On her left hand were the chunky rings that she wore, and the ones that encircled her arms, knees, and ankles had not fallen off. Through her half-open mouth the moon was reflected on the circle of her still damp teeth. Its reflection was like the trail of light left by the soul when it flies up to the turey.[17]

At her feet, Caonareyto gazed upon her angrily. Dry-eyed and barely conscious of his terrible misfortune, he distractedly clasped his chest with his arms.

Once the funeral procession was assembled the ceremony began. They performed the dance of death. In a tender and emotional dirge Caonareyto lamented his misfortune, the virtues of the dead girl, and his soul's despair. At that moment, rhythmic sobbing accompanied the strange requiem. Mournful gasps rose to a murmur. The sound of the whistles was a doleful plaint. A mysterious incense rose from the gentle breeze filled with the smell of the sea, from the mystical veil of the vaporous moonlight and from human sadness. The behíque, fasting, drew near with a preparation of intoxicating herbs. A murmur arose like prayers or salutations, like silence that is really an entreaty or cries that are really sobbing. They began to make their offerings to the priest (baskets full of cakes, pieces of which were distributed to those present). He asked the Cemí:[18] "What does the death of the maiden portend?"

The crowd waited in awe. After a while, the minister, rising from his attitude of prostration, proclaimed the terrifying prophecy: "Aritjuma, Aritjuma! (White men will come to your land)." The people looked up at Nonum and turned to the Ti,[19] and they began to dance with wild abandon the Igi aya bougbe (We'd rather die than be slaves).

The following day, Caonareyto wept his elegy at the foot of Bayacu's raised tomb. He invoked the four stars Racuno, Savaco, Achinao, and Coromo. He asked Louquo, the Great Power, for strength and knelt, resting the haft of his arrow on the ground. He bent over and let himself fall forward onto it. It passed right through him as he fervently murmured: "Bayacú, Bayacú, my dear one."

Yareya

Yareya was beautiful. She was as pretty as the pitahaya[20] flower, as pure as a dove, and as graceful as the guaní.[21] The fire of the tropical noonday burned in her eyes that were as black as the cloak of mist in which the night wraps itself and as bright as the twinkling evening star. Her body was as supple as the reeds in the lagoons. It swayed in graceful undulating movements like the flowers in the morning breeze or like the palm tree on the plain in the pleasant gusts of the afternoon wind. The breeze imbibed its fragrance from her silky black hair just as the air absorbs the harmonies of a May afternoon.

Everyone bowed down before Yareya. From the peaceful edges of the Yariguá to the high green banks of the Cauto, everyone loved her. When Yareya went out of her cansí[22] her tiny footprints pressed on carpets of velvety moss covered with little flowers. The Indians wove lovely garlands to adorn her brow.

One afternoon, when the sun had not yet hidden beneath the horizon, long before Columbus's ships reached the Bay of Sabinal, at the hour when, in a thousand different ways, the wonders of nature gravitate toward that mysterious region and when no bird, bough, or leaf draws breath, Yareya, a ray of light reflected on her brow with its fine wreath of white and blue feathers, made her way slowly toward the banks of the wide Cauto. She looked at the reflection of her lovely face in the moving mirror of the waters and found herself so pure and so beautiful that she allowed a slight smile to appear on her lips, and a flush tinged the roses in her cheeks. She smiled like the morning in the first rays of sunlight. From her enticing mouth, a mansion of pearls and wallflowers, came a sigh that was carried on the rose-colored wings of the afternoon breeze to perfume the flowers. She fixed her almond-shaped eyes on the expanse of water and, in a voice sweeter than the murmur of palm trees and the playing of an Aeolian harp, exclaimed: "How late he is!"

Barely had the beautiful Cuban uttered these impatient words than the sound of oars could be heard on the water. Suddenly, a simple canoe appeared in a mass of spume. A proud Indian leaped ashore. His head was adorned with magnificent guatinî[23] feathers. A bow and arrow hung from his shoulders that were tanned by the burning rays of the sun. Gold and precious stones were magnificently displayed on the brave Guacanayabo, chief of the province of the same name. They did not speak, but an echo of "I adore you!" full of passion and perfume, rose on the air and was lost in the solitude of the jungle.

"Yareya, goddess of my thoughts, soul of my soul, are you sad? Perhaps Mabuya has taken hold of your spirit?"

"Be quiet, my love, I know that you are the bravest man in the eastern province; everyone has disarmed their bows and lain down their clubs before you. Everyone fears and loves you. You can shoot the arrow more powerfully than lightning from the clouds, but even you cannot ease my sorrow; you cannot banish my tears."

"What's wrong? Why are you so upset, beautiful lily

of the valley?"

"I don't know, but when I came to these shores that witnessed our first excitement and pure love, where I spent the happy days of my childhood, I felt my soul become sad when I heard the melancholy song of the cucubá[24] in the dovecotes. A premonition as black as your eyes has entered my heart. An evil spirit tells me that soon the waters of this river will be stained with the blood of your warriors. The wings of mourning of the goddess of evil hover over my head. Oh Guacanayabo, many, many sorrows await me!"

"Be calm, Yareya. Know that your sad news fills my soul with a terrible dread. Your laments are mine; your sorrows are my sorrows, for I love you, Yareya. You are enthroned in my soul; you shimmer in my loving heart like the moonlight shimmers on the crystal waters of this river. You are my heaven, and if the sky of my happiness clouds over, everything will appear sad and ugly. You are weeping; oh do not weep, no. Hold back your tears; do not speak of your premonitions. Do not hurt our love with them. Let us not allow our hopes to fade as we shall offend heaven and earth. And even if this does come to pass, will you always love me as I love you?"

"Always!"

The moon illuminated the green expanses. Fireflies glimmered in the undergrowth. A gentle breeze scented the fields and rustled the treetops. It was one of those Cuban nights that speak to the soul and that are the delight of this enchanting pearl of an island. The calm waters of the mighty Cauto were churned by a host of canoes and guairos[25] carrying many Indian warriors from the tribe of the chief of Jiguaní. They were armed with arrows and stout guayacán[26] clubs. They had come at the command of the cruel Ornofay. Desirous of Yareya's love, he was determined to abduct her even if it meant shedding the blood of his men.

Suddenly the sound of a guamo shell echoed from valley to valley, disturbing the silence of the night. It was the signal to begin fighting. The only thing heard throughout the region was the conch sounding the battle hymn. A legion of handsome warriors sent by the brave Guacanayabo hastened to stop the march of the invaders. It was a terrible battle! All that was heard was the sound of clubs cracking skulls and of bodies rolling on the sand, the battle cries of the combatants and the mournful lament of those who had fallen and were near to death. The battlefield was a lake of steaming blood. The countless bodies offered a sumptuous feast for the birds of prey.

"Where is Yareya?" asked the bloodthirsty Ornofay in the midst of the fighting. "Bring her to me; bring her to me!"

Suddenly a proud Indian broke through the crowd and, going up to the terrible Ornofay, he said: "Mighty warrior, you have come under cover of night to bring death to a defenseless tribe. What is it that you want?"

The Indian retorted: "I want the sun of suns, the beautiful lily of this valley, the lovely Yareya, whose charms have captured my heart."

"Yareya! She who has joined her being to mine, her soul to my soul? Come, let death, the angel of extermination, decide between us."

And they threw themselves on each other.

In the morning, when the first rays of the sun began to tinge the lofty peaks of the distant mountains purple and gold, Yareya contemplated the scene of the battle. She was confused and trembling like a young bird that peers out of its nest for the first time, sees at its feet the huge green abyss, and does not dare to measure the space with its feeble wings. She moaned piteously and turned to look at the remains of the battle. She searched for her lover among the dead! There, covered in blood, lay the cruel Ornofay and a few feet away the handsome Guacanayabo, who was dying. When she saw him, the lovesick Yareya threw herself on him frantically, her black hair loose in the wind.

"Guacanayabo, wake up. It is your faithful, loving Yareya! Gentle breezes of the forest and of the river, tell Guacanayabo to wake up, that Yareya is still alive but is dying of a broken heart."

The Indian stirred and opened his eyes. Yareya planted a torrent of passionate kisses on his lips.

"Do you still love me, Yareya?" the dying lover asked, gripping the young woman's hand.

"Do I love you! Look, I love you more than my soul. You are my life, Guacanayabo, the ray of light the lights up my existence. If your life is ended I will die like the flowers when the sun's rays do not give them life. I love you as the green palm groves love the murmur of the April breezes. I love you as the birds love the solitary places of the jungle. I adore you as they adore the Cemí. No other lips shall ever rest on my troubled breast."

The Indian woman was silent. Guacanayabo fixed his faltering gaze on her. Yareya bent her head over the chief's face. And a kiss, the last one for these loving souls, broke the ominous silence of the battlefield. Guacanayabo had died! Yareya was no more!

According to tradition, on the nights of the full moon when the banks of the Cauto rest in silence, a light canoe covered with flowers may be seen on its clear waters. A woman climbs out, casting her sad sighs to the wind. The ghost stops beside a grave that is shaded perpetually by flowering camellias. She kisses the green grass deliriously. Then she runs away, crying in a pathetic voice,

"I love you! I still adore you!" The old Indians claim that the ghost is the lovesick Yareya, and on winter nights around the fire, they tell their children this tradition that the murmuring waves of the turbulent Cauto still seem to repeat.

The Yumurí Pass

The pass through the beautiful Yumurí valley has one of the most interesting legends. This is an ancient legend about two young Indians and the formation of the pass of the beautiful Yumurí, the crystalline river that bears that name. The protagonists are the daughter of a chief of the western region and the heir to the great Siboney chieftaincy of Camagüey, who lived hundreds of kilometers apart.

The legend tells how, when little Coalina was born, her father celebrated the birth with much feasting, areítos, and merriment. When the dancing was at its liveliest, an ancient behíque, a stranger to them all, appeared before the chief and said: "You are celebrating the birth, and everything will go well, but come the day that she falls in love, disaster will overtake your village."

"Why is that?" asked the chief suspiciously, but the man disappeared into the spirals of the Indian tobacco smoke.

At first the young chief was puzzled by the prophecy but, seeing his little daughter in her mother's lap, he smiled at his young wife. However, she could not forget that apparent prophecy. The years passed, and it seemed to the mother that they went by more quickly. She feared the onset of her beloved Coalina's adolescence for she saw how she was growing and becoming ever more lovely, arousing admiration in the men of the chief's household. One day, sighing and weeping, she pointed this out to her husband the chief. She feared the time was coming when Coalina would fall in love. The chief, suddenly alarmed, recalled the fatal prophecy of the strange behíque who was never seen again and whom nobody knew.

After a sleepless night he decided to build a caney[27] for Coalina on top of a mountain that overlooked his valley. That would be the convent where he would lock up the beauty of his adored adolescent daughter. No man would be able to climb up there on pain of death. When the caney was built, he made his daughter go there, whence she would never be allowed to climb down or to see any man. He assigned many Indian women to watch over her. They were sufficiently old that they no longer thought of romance. Thus they would accurately shoot at any man who attempted to approach the lovely Coalina.

The young girl lived happily with her guardians, who adored her. They found her the most delicious fruit and in spring the prettiest fireflies that adorned her ebony hair like flowers of light. By day they decorated her with the most colorful flowers.

Coalina often saw her mother, who brought her lovely skirts made from bright guacamaya and tocoloro[28] feathers. She was happy, she was growing like a lovely wildflower, and she dressed and adorned herself like the most beautiful Indian princess.

Word of Coalina's beauty reached Nerey, the son of the Siboney chief. Although he had heard of the mysterious behíque's prophecy, this did not deter him, and he wished to meet the cloistered virgin. The young Camagüey Indian set out for Yumurí, where the beautiful Coalina lived. He walked day and night without stopping, taking only short rests.

He was strong. His bronze, resilient, and beautiful body did not know fatigue. He crossed the vast plain, climbed hills, waded across rivers, and then crossed yet more plains and climbed more mountains. When the full moon had risen only a few hours, he made out on the top of a mountain, the caney of the beautiful Coalina. There she remained, no Indian man having dared to approach her. Everyone feared the prophecy of the unknown behíque.

Hiding himself here and crawling there, Nerey came near to the caney of the beautiful girl whom he loved without ever having seen her. The guardians had never had to shoot their arrows, as no Indian of their tribe dreamed of approaching the dwelling of the young woman who was taboo for them. But the Camagüey Indian was not afraid of the arrows, nor did he fear the clubs. He felt strongly attracted to that lovely young woman who, unaware of his presence, was moving toward a beautiful firefly to the right of where he lay hidden in a bush.

How beautiful the Indian virgin of the bronze body was! She wore a crown of fragrant white wallflowers in which, like living candles that light up dark nights, shone the fireflies that abound here and that Puerto Ricans call cucabanos. They came irresistibly close to each other. She saw only the living light. He was looking at the beauty illuminated by the moon and did not notice the guardian who saw him only when he stood up and cried out: "Coalina, beautiful flower of the Yumurí. I have come so far to see you."

"Who are you, please?" she asked curiously.

"I am Nerey, the future chief of Camagüey."

"Nerey, a lovely name. Is your Camagüey very far away?"

It is some moons to visit your tribe, but no time at all to see you, lovely flower of this place, beautiful star of heaven."

"Oh, how delightfully you speak, Nerey, brave chief of Camagüey."

When she heard this, the guardian remembered the ominous prophecy about when Coalina would fall in love. Letting out a cry, she began to run toward the valley, shouting: "Coalina has fallen in love!"

"Coalina, my turtledove, bright tocoloro, I love you and I want you to give me a son who will be the chief of my Camagüey."

"Oh Nerey, Nerey!" cried the Indian virgin, deeply moved. The mountain trembled.

"Come here, my Coalina, darling of my love, let me hold you in my arms, beautiful pitahaya flower!"

"But what language is this, which I have never before heard?" inquired the maiden.

"It is the language of love, Coalina, the love that I feel for you!"

"This is love?" the Indian maiden sighed again, gazing at the bronzed handsome fellow. The mountain trembled.

"It is love, it is love, Coalina is in love," echoed the remaining guardians, and, without shooting an arrow or seizing a club, they ran down the mountain behind the valley.

"Come into my arms, pretty flower of the tibisí!"[29]

"Tell me, Nerey, fine Indian man! Is this love that I feel fluttering in my breast, just like the mountain that trembles?" the innocent Indian virgin asked, alarmed.

"Yes, Coalina, it is love," answered the proud Indian. The young woman sighed deeply. The earth shook. She lifted her eyes to heaven, and there on top of the mountain stood the old white-haired behíque, who was smiling.

Coalina, startled, ran into the strong arms of the Indian, who embraced her. At that moment, the earth shook, and the mountain split in two, sweeping them away. The river's raging current rushed through the gap and it carried the lovers along with it.

This is the origin of the inlet of Yumurí, according to the legend. Be sure that, on the nights of the full moon, you can hear the wind blowing through the gap, murmuring "Coalina ... Nerey ... Coalina ... Nerey ..."

The Legend of Canímar (2)

Canímar was a handsome Indian. He was called Canímar like the deep river beside which lay the chiefdom where he was born and lived happily until the Spaniards came to colonize that part of the Matanzas region. In the same chiefdom of Canímar lived a very lovely maiden called Flor de Caney. She was the darling of her parents and admired by all who laid eyes on her. Canímar adored her and longed to make her his wife. But one of the leaders of the Spanish conquistadors came with arquebus and sword and, after capturing the territory and all its Indians, he noticed Flor de Caney's beauty and took her home with him.

The lovesick Canímar was in great despair, and the unhappy Flor de Caney was immensely sad and distressed. Often in the twilight hour, the beautiful Indian would hear, mingled with the plaintive cooing of the tojosa, the even more sorrowful complaint of the Siboney on the other side of the river. It was a song full of nostalgia. But sometimes her lord and master would also hear that song and send a pack of hounds in that direction. However, the Indian, as quick as a flash, slid down the steep riverbank and reached safety swimming in the cold water of the river.

One fine evening, the lovely girl heard her lover's lament and

went toward the sound of his voice to beg him to flee forever from that place where his life was in danger. They sat together on the riverbank.

"Go far away from me; I am a caged bird," she said.

"I cannot leave you, Flor de Caney."

"But here you will meet your death, my love."

"I prefer to meet my death close to you."

"Now you shall have your wish, Indian dog," said the lord and master. And, taking the weapon from his treacherous servant, he fired at the chest of the Indian who had turned around when he heard his voice.

The Indian rolled into the river. At that moment, a loud cry rent the air: "I'm going with you, Canímar!" and the beautiful Indian flung herself into the river after her lover, and the dark green water swallowed their remains. She had rather the dark waters of the Canímar unite her with her lover's remains than stay at the side of the man who had murdered him.

Today a fine bridge stands like a cenotaph overlooking the broad Canímar that separated them in life and united them in death. Looking up at the steep cliffs from the magnificent bridge, it seems as if the air moans and wails over the green waters, and one can hear the Indian's sorrowful cry: "I'm going with you, Canímar!"

The Heroic Martyr

In the heroic region of Oriente lived an Indian couple who had a seven-year-old daughter who looked like a little copper statue. When the conquistadors came, the Indian man, along with a group of others, fought to defend their territory. It was not long before they were killed, but the chief, dodging their arrows, managed to elude them until he was finally caught by a pack of the white men's hounds. His unhappy wife, her child in her arms, watched from the top of a dagame[31] tree as he was torn apart by the ferocious dogs. She swore to take revenge on the conquistadors.

For a time the Indian woman used her sling to hurl down from the heights of the Sierra Maestra stones that fatally hit their target: Spaniards crossing the valleys. Time passed, and she lived in the hills like a mountain goat, finding food for herself and her daughter, who was now grown. They ate whatever they could find and wrought havoc on the Spaniards.

But the day came when the mother and daughter were taken prisoner during an ambush. She was judged and sentenced to be hanged so that her body swinging from the tree would serve as a warning to the indigenous rebels. But the beautiful little Indian girl became the property of the leader.

"Why don't you sentence my daughter?" she asked.

"No, I won't kill your daughter," the leader said. "She is for me."

"Very well, keep her for yourself, but let her come to me now so that I can say good-bye and embrace her for the last time."

The girl did not wait for their permission but ran, weeping, into her mother's arms. The Indian woman held her in her arms and spoke tenderly in her ear. Eager to carry out the sentence, they immediately rushed to seize her, but when they tried to tear her away, the mother opened her arms and said: "There you have the part of her that interests you; her soul will rise up to the turey with her parents." And the girl's body fell lifeless to the ground. Her mother had smothered her in her arms rather than let her be taken to the conquistadors.

Guanaroca

To the southeast of the beautiful bay of Cienfuegos stretches a saltwater lagoon into which flow the waters of the River Arimao. It is the lagoon of Guanaroca, on whose still surface the pale moon is reflected, the sweet Maroya of the Siboneys, that makes the dew and is the benign patroness of love.

According to Siboney legend, the Guanaroca lagoon is the manifestation of the moon on earth. Do you know that poetic tradition, reader? It has a natural, primitive quality that is very typical of the simple beliefs of men who lived in direct contact with wild, untamed, and abundant nature.

In times long past, Huión, the sun, periodically left the cave where he sheltered to rise up into the sky and light Ocon, the earth that was fertile and bountiful but still empty of human beings. Huión had a wish: to create man so that he would have someone to admire and worship him, to await his appearance each day and to see him as the powerful lord of heat, light, and life.

Huión's magic spell created Hamao, the first man. Now the sun had someone to worship him, to greet him every morning with respectful joy from the happy valleys and the high mountains. This was enough for Huión, and he did not concern himself anymore with Hamao. For Hamao, the great love he felt for his creator was not enough to fill his heart. He felt lonely in the midst of abundant nature, provided with luxuriant vegetation, populated with creatures that came together to love each other. In the midst of the universal display of life and love, Hamao felt his spirit languish, and the pointlessness of his lonely life distressed him.

The sensitive, gentle Maroya, the moon, felt sorry for Hamao. To sweeten his existence she gave him a companion, creating Guanaroca, or the first woman. The first man's happiness was great. At last he had someone with whom he could share enjoyment and sorrow, happiness and sadness, play and work. The two loved each other deliriously, with unlimited passion, not yet having wearied of it. From their union was born Imao, the first child.

Guanaroca, a mother at last, bestowed all her affection on her son. The father, jealous and feeling left out, devised the criminal plan of abducting him. One night, taking advantage of Guanaroca's sleep, he seized the tender infant and took him into the forest. The excessive heat and starvation killed the frail child. In order to conceal his crime the father took a large gourd, made a hole in it, and put the cold body of the infant inside. Then he hung the gourd from the branch of a tree.

When Guanaroca awoke and noticed the absence of her husband and son, she rushed out to look for him. She wandered anxiously through the wood, calling to her loved ones in vain. She was ready to fall down, exhausted, when the raucous cry of a black bird, probably the judío,[32] made her lift her head and notice the gourd that was hanging from the branch of a nearby tree. Either because of the innate curiosity that was already apparent in the first woman or a strange premonition, Guanaroca felt compelled to climb the tree and take down the gourd.

She noticed that it had a hole in it. Frightened, she thought she could see the body of her adored son inside it. She was so distressed and overcome with emotion that she fainted, and the gourd fell out her hands onto the ground. As it broke, she watched in amazement as out of the gourd came fish, different-sized tortoises, and a huge amount of liquid that spilled all the way down the hill.

Then came the great wonder that Guanaroca would behold: the fish turned into the rivers that flow through the territory of Jagua, the biggest tortoise became the Majagua peninsula and the others, in order of size, became the other keys. The hot, salty tears of the wretched mother who inconsolably lamented the death of her beloved son formed the lagoon and delta that bear her name: Guanaroca.

Jagua

The jealousy sowed in his heart by the god of evil caused Hamao to feel the first pain. With the loss of her son, Guanaroca experienced the first and deepest sorrow a mother can suffer. Too late, Hamao realized how irrational his jealousy had been and began to understand a father's love. Guanaroca forgave him, and from forgiveness came their second son: Canimao.

His childhood was peaceful and happy under the constant care of his affectionate mother. The child became a man, and he began to be filled with a vague anxiety, a deep sadness. He was not able to understand his state of mind that made him lose interest in life.

One day, returning to his lonely hut, he stopped to watch two little birds that were caressing on the branch of a tree. Then he understood the reason for his sorrow. He was alone in the world. He had no companion to caress and to be caressed by, to whom he could tell his sorrows, joys, hopes, and dreams. There was only one woman on earth, but that was Guanaroca, who had given him life.

Wandering through the fields, he tried in vain to take his mind off his loneliness. He spotted a leafy tree, quite tall and with a rounded top. Fruit hung in abundance from its branches, large oval-shaped fruit, brownish-gray in color. Many of them were ripe and fell from the tree onto the ground. Some had burst open to reveal a fleshy interior full of tiny seeds. Canimao had an irresistible desire to taste that fruit. Picking one of the ripest, he bit into it greedily. It had a bittersweet taste. As it was pleasing to the palate, he found a plentiful supply of free food in that strange delicacy that nature offered in abundance.

He liked it so much that he went to his hut to fetch a palm basket, intending to fill it with the strange fruit that he found delicious. When he returned, Canimao began to pile them into a heap. He was about to put them into the basket when a ray of moonlight struck the fruit that was piled up anyhow, causing a marvelous being of the opposite sex to appear. It was a very young, beautiful, and smiling woman. She had a finely shaped figure, and her velvety skin was golden. She had large, tender, caressing eyes, a red smiling mouth, and long, very black and abundant hair.

Canimao looked at her with increasing rapture. He felt that sadness and melancholy were fleeing from his heart as if by magic, driven out by happiness and love. No longer would he travel the road of life alone. He had someone to love and to love him.

That beautiful companion who had appeared from the pile of ripe fruit that was struck by a ray of moonlight, was a present from Maroya, the goddess of the night. Just as she had ended the loneliness of Hamao, the first man, by sending him Guanaroca, she also wished to brighten their son Canimao's existence by presenting him with the gift of another woman.

From the first moment Canimao loved her with all the passion of his young heart that hungered for caresses. He made her his, and she became the mother of his children. That second woman was called Jagua, a word meaning wealth, source, spring, fountain, or beginning. And the tree from whose fruit the woman had emerged was also called jagua, and for that reason it was considered sacred.

Jagua, Canimao's wife, was the one who handed out laws to the natural and peaceful Siboneys. She taught them to fish and hunt, to till the fields, how to sing and dance, and how to cure diseases.

Guanaroca was the mother of the first men. Jagua was the mother of the first women. The sons of Guanaroca, Canimao's mother, had children by the daughters of Jagua, and all human beings on earth are descended from those first couples.

According to the Dominican tradition, Cihualohuatl, the snake woman was the mythological Eve who gave birth to children two by two, male and female, so as to facilitate the reproduction and preservation of the species. Siboney tradition is more "normal." Guanaroca, the Cuban Eve, has only male children, and Jagua, the second Eve, only female, and they then form couples in order to reproduce.

 # The Wicked Indian Woman

The cult of the dead is very ancient and widespread. We find it in many different forms among primitive peoples, depending on the level of development or civilization they have attained. One might say that the most rudimentary manifestation of a cult to those who have passed away marks the first sign of nationhood in a people.

As is natural, having acquired a certain level of cultural development, the Siboneys had the custom of honoring the dead, whom they imagined lived beyond the grave. They had quite original ideas about the spirits of the dead. The shade or ghost of a dead person was called operito. This would appear to the living in human form. Its only physical difference from humans was that it did not have a navel. This is why, at night, if an Indian sensed that someone was lying in his hammock, he would pass his hand over the abdomen to find out if it was a living or a dead person.

The soul or spirit of the dead person in its intangible or ethereal form was called the Hupia. While the person was alive, the soul or spirit was called Goeiz.

It was the custom among the Siboneys to offer fruit to the dead. The Jagua Indians preferred the fruit of the bagá, a tree that was plentiful along those muddy coasts and lands. They used its wood for making floats or corks to hold up their fishing nets, as fishermen in that part of Cuba still do today. The fruit of the bagá is not very pleasant to eat, but the Siboneys, considering that the dead should not be too demanding where food is concerned, offered it to them with the best of intentions, believing that they were doing them good.

A tree that served them so well, both materially and spiritually, obviously had to be considered sacred by the simple Siboneys, and they cultivated it carefully. Even today the bagá abounds along the coasts and some rivers in Cuba. The fruit is used for feeding livestock. Fishermen still use its light, porous roots to float their nets in the water. But when the Siboneys died out and their place was taken by more civilized races, the bagá lost its role in providing food for the souls of the dead. Nowadays we are happy to offer them flowers. Every year, at the times when the bagá bore fruit most abundantly, the Siboneys would hold communal religious ceremonies to commemorate the dead. They went in a procession to the huts of the dead or cemeteries, carrying huge baskets of bagá fruit, which they left there with the greatest respect.

Apart from these ceremonies of a general nature, they used to celebrate others individually or in families, offering the said fruit to their deceased relatives and also to the chiefs, behíques, and warriors. These offerings were made more out of fear than reverence, as they believed that the dead wandered through the fields, valleys, forests, and villages at night and could cause harm.

There was a beautiful Indian called Iasiga—and here begins the legend—the lawful wife of a hardworking Siboney known as Maitio. They lived in perfect peace and total harmony that was only occasionally disturbed by slight clouds in the sky of domestic happiness. While he went away to devote himself to hunting and fishing, she prepared meals, took care of the sowing, wove nets and baskets, and performed all the duties of an industrious woman.

Iasiga had an ardent and passionate nature. She loved her husband but not enough to only have eyes for him. Indeed, the first time she saw Gaguiano, a handsome Siboney who liked to taste the fruit of other people's orchards, she felt such intense passion for him that she forgot the trusting Maitio and succumbed without resisting, enjoying the pleasures of forbidden love as if tomorrow would never come.

Often when he came home Maitio would notice his wife's absence. When she came back she apologized, saying she had gone to offer bagá fruit to her dead relatives when in fact she was returning from her illicit excursions.

In this world, everything must come to an end, and Maitio's trustingness was no exception. One afternoon, on the way back to his hut, a cruel suspicion seized his guileless soul. When he reached the empty house, instead of waiting patiently he asked his neighbors if they had seen Iasiga. They told him they had seen her go by with a tray of bagá, a sure sign that she was going to visit the dead. This did not stop Maitio worrying. He went to the nearby riverbank and set off in his canoe for the cemetery. From afar he could make out a couple in tender conversation on the beach. His heart missed a beat. He was afraid that his suspicion would become harsh reality. He rowed with renewed effort and finally managed to land without being seen. He advanced cautiously and appeared suddenly before the unsuspecting and confident lovers, who were none other than Iasiga and Gaguiano.

The cowardly lover fled, and a loud cry of anguish escaped

from her breast. Maitio, his face twisted with grief, went up to her and said in a hoarse voice: "May you be cursed a thousand times, lying woman. May Mabuya punish your infidelity by condemning you to wander eternally along the coast, never to rest nor arouse compassion."

At that moment, the unfaithful Iasiga was turned into a sea monster. It appears from time to time, silent and sad, beseeching the solitary fishermen who make a living from the sea in their boats or canoes. That is how the legend goes, anyway. Nowadays many people believe that the creature who gave rise to the tradition really exists. Some think it is the manatee that comes to the waters of the Jucaral or an enormous turtle or tortoise that enters Jagua bay.

The Mulatas

An excessive fondness for dancing, ballgames, liquor they brewed from fermented maize, and their habitual licentiousness had completely corrupted the customs of the Jagua Siboneys. The areítos or popular folk festivals that took place on the outskirts of the villages were held one after another. Now no one bothered to tend the farmland or smallholdings, nor to sow at new moon, the most propitious time. Soon they began to suffer from hunger and famine as a result of the scarcity of maize, cassava, sweet potato, and other foodstuffs that were their staples. Raids by neighboring Indians made the situation worse. They laid waste to the fields in a warlike manner, destroyed the countryside, and took the women captive. The men, weakened by ease and licentiousness, were not brave enough to free the native land from the invaders.

The old headman, anxious to find a solution to so many troubles, called together the council of behíques and elders. After a lengthy and unhurried discussion, they decided to consult the Cemí or idol so that it would indicate the best way to end the devastation that threatened to destroy the country.

The Cemí was consulted with the required ceremony. It revealed that the cause of so many evils was the beauty and seduc-

tive singing and dancing of the women, especially those of the chief's court. Their grace and supple movement in the singing and dancing of the areítos made them stand out. The solution was to make those women disappear. The chief, behíques, and elders met again in council. With great sorrow, but resigning themselves to the inevitable, they agreed to kill the seven singers and dancers of the court and thus completely root out the problem, as the idol had advised.

When the behíques and the chief went to do what they had agreed, they did not have the courage to kill them. They decided to exile them to an island in the south. Some think it was Grand Cayman, but it most believe it was the little island in the Bay of Jagua, known today as Cayo Carenas.

In order to avoid tiresome scenes of despair and weeping they kept this most inviolable secret. The most astute of the behíques used false promises and flattery to make them think they were going on an outing to the next little island. Trusting and happy, they prepared to embark in the canoe that would take them there along with the behíque.

Once at sea and heading south in search of the island, the behíque noticed that there were only six women in the canoe. One was missing. It was Aycayía, the prettiest. According to her companions, she must have stayed behind adorning herself and arrived too late to embark. As the behíque was thinking of going back to land to look for the woman they had left behind, strong gusts of wind began to blow and seemed to rage more violently that afternoon. The frail canoe, a plaything of the angry god of the winds, glided rapidly down the choppy waves until it was capsized by an extremely violent gust of wind. The six unfortunate dancers drowned, but the behíque, a good swimmer, managed to reach the shore. He did not attempt to save even one of them.

The god of the waters turned the shipwrecked Indian women into mermaids. Ever since then they live happily and playfully in the water, entertaining and lulling fishermen and sailors with their melodious singing. On days when there are strong winds, they appear on the choppy waves and delight in startling those who dare to ply the waters of the sea of Jagua in frail boats. The fishermen and sailors call them the Mulatas.

Aycayía

Six of the seven beautiful singers and dancers of the chief's entourage died in the shipwreck of the canoe. The one who escaped death—either because of her unintentional delay in hanging about performing her toilet or because she had previously been warned by the behíque, whose special favorite she was—was called Aycayía. She was the most beautiful of the seven, the one who danced most gracefully and had the sweetest and most melodious voice. Thus it was no surprise that she continued to disturb the peace of the community alone, keeping the men from their work and the warriors from performing their duties, and bringing disharmony to homes.

The chief, elders, and behíques met once more in council and agreed to consult the all-powerful Cemí for a second time. It spoke to them thus: "Aycayía is sin incarnate, the sin of beauty, art, and love. She gives pleasure to men but makes them her slaves and robs them of their will. And her diabolical power is such that, by pleasing all, she gives herself to no one. She is a virgin and she will die a virgin. If you want to live in peace, cast her from your bosom."

They followed the Cemí's advice. Aycayía was condemned to

live away from society with an old woman called Guanayoa for company. She was taken to a remote place, known today as Punta Majagua. Unfortunately, this did not improve the situation. Such was the power that the beautiful dancer exercised over men that the Siboneys went to Punta Majagua every day. They abandoned their work and their homes just to see Aycayía perform her wonderful dances with her extraordinary agility and talent and to hear her sing in her sweet, caressing voice. Naturally they all vied in presenting her with gifts, bringing her fruit, feathers, shells, gold leaf, and other ornaments to satisfy feminine vanity. She smiled at everyone and accepted gifts from them all, without any one being able to boast of being her favorite.

The poor women of Jagua felt abandoned, the married ones by their husbands, the maidens by their sweethearts, who only had eyes and ears for the incomparable Aycayía. They went to the chief to complain, and he took the matter to the senior behíque, who tried in vain to make the strayed sheep return to the fold. The beautiful exile was more than a match for any threats or inducements.

The behíque then went to the supreme and infallible resource— he consulted the Cemí of the goddess Jagua for the third time. She gave him some little black seeds along with the following instructions: "These seeds are a charm against forgetting and unhappiness. Give them to the women to plant in their orchards. When they bloom, their concerns and anguish will cease and they will regain the affection of their sweethearts and husbands."

From the seeds carefully planted the women grew the tree known today as the majagua or demajagua, which means "of Mother Jagua." Ever since then, its leaves, flowers, and wood are considered to be a charm that prevents conjugal infidelity.

The trees grew, and when their first flowers bloomed, a violent hurricane arose suddenly. It swept away the tall house across the water where Aycayía and her elderly companion lived, and the stormy waves dragged the two women into the sea. The young woman was turned into an undine or mermaid, and the old woman into a turtle. Thus the ill-fated and destructive reign of the incomparable and beautiful Aycayía over the Jagua Siboneys was ended.

The tradition is not clear about what became of Aycayía at sea. Some suppose her to be a solitary undine that wanders around the bay of Jagua or in the open sea, blowing on an enormous mother-of-pearl shell, the great shell of our Antillean seas whose rasping sound mingles with that of Caorao, the god of the storm. Others believe she is not alone but rides on Guanayoca, now a huge and repulsive turtle, still blowing on the shell, condemned to wander perpetually through the rough seas, atoning for the sin of having been on earth, beautiful, seductive, and a virgin.

The Battle of the Canoes

Once the wayward Aycayía disappeared, peace, industry, and respectability reigned once more among the Jagua Indians. The tilled fields, the forests, and the sea provided vegetables, birds, and fish. No longer did the raids by hostile tribes inspire terror. The Jaguans were ready to defend their beloved native lares in the forests and valleys or on the water with their arrowheads and clubs.

The chief, elders, and behíques were very pleased with this radical change. They saw the protecting hand of the Cemí in the benefits received. For their part, the industrious Indian women continued carefully watering the majagua, the tree that protected conjugal fidelity.

However, the Jagua Siboneys did not completely abandon their parties and pastimes. From time to time they played their batos or ballgames on the outskirts of the village. There were two opposing teams who threw a ball made of resin from one to the other. The players hit it in the air with their hands or legs. From time to time they held areítos to celebrate important events, but they tried not to overdo such feasts as they could have an enervating effect. Instead, they frequently reenacted the exploits of the fierce

Ornoya. On more than one occasion, his bravery and mettle had been put to the test in bloody combat with enemy Indians, and he gained a well-deserved reputation as a skilful and invincible warrior. Whenever the native soil was threatened with attack, the chief nominated Ornoya the leader of the warriors who would repel the aggressors.

Ornocoy, the principal chief of one of the Lucaya islands, was an old fox who was very experienced in the art of war, pillage, and plunder. He was eager to add to his loot and his number of captive women. He organized a piratical expedition to the port of Jagua, whose inhabitants had a reputation for indolence, preferring the pleasures of singing and dancing to the severity of war. He gathered his people, well armed with bows and arrows, spears and clubs and, embarking them into twenty long and swift canoes, set out for Jagua. The voyage was difficult and arduous on account of the wild sea that toyed with the fragile boats. But the Lucayos were as skilled at sailing as they were at fighting, and, battling constantly against the elements, they reached the beaches of Jagua. They enter its port resolutely, canoes in double file. They brandished their arms above their heads, the war rattles sounded, and the air echoed with their battle cries.

In one of the first canoes stood the old and powerfully-built Chief Ornocoy, his body painted black and red. Elegant feathers streamed from his head, and his eyes flashed. On his back he carried a quiver full of arrows, the bow hung from his waist, and he carried a gnarled club in his right hand. He led his men calmly and serenely, certain of victory.

The cry of alarm spread among the Siboney village, and the peaceful inhabitants were seized with fear at the unexpected appearance of the fierce Lucayos. The Indian mothers ran to their huts; taking their tender children they hid in the clefts of the mountains while the men ran to and fro indecisively. The old chief, seeing there was no time to lose, called for the fierce Ornoya. "Ornocoy's men have come here for battle," he said, "to steal our property and our women once they have killed us. Our salvation is in your hands. There are the warriors. Lead them to victory or to death."

Ornoya replied haughtily: "I swear by the goddess of Jagua that I will send the chief of the Lucayos to the bottom of the sea or die in the attempt." He immediately ran to the beach where the armed but indecisive warriors awaited him. They dragged the canoes into the sea and climbed into them agilely. The conch shells sounded, and the men brandished spears and clubs, uttering defiant cries as they advanced to meet the enemy.

Ornoya also led and rallied his men. His proud figure stood out with its bronzed skin. His head was adorned with blue and white feathers, and in his right hand was a sturdy club.

It was a terrible skirmish. The canoes collide, and Lucayos and Siboneys set upon each other with spear thrusts and blows from their clubs. The dead and wounded fell to the bottom of the vessels or into the sea. Some canoes were overturned. Their occupants continued fighting furiously in the water. The battle continued relentless and undecided for a long time. The invading chief urged his men on and set them an example of bravery. He brandished his fearful club with exceptional skill, splitting open an enemy skull with each blow. Ornoya matched him in bravery and strength, having youth on his side. Enraged at the ongoing battle and wishing to bring it to a speedy conclusion, he went resolutely to meet the fearsome chief. He maneuvered the canoe and managed to get near to that of the Lucayo chief. He confronted him and challenged him to single combat. They set upon each other fiercely with the clubs. With a swift movement, Ornoya dodged a blow from the old warrior and with a leap, hurled himself into the enemy canoe. Raising his club high, he brought it down heavily on the head of the cruel Chief Ornocoy, who wobbled and fell, his skull shattered into a hundred pieces.

The death of the chief made the Lucayos lose heart while the Siboneys, roused by the example of Ornoya, who spread terror and death like an angel of destruction, redoubled their efforts until they achieved total victory. The enemy canoes that had not been smashed or overturned attempted to escape but were followed and captured. More than two hundred were taken prisoner, among them six chiefs.

Ornoya gave the order to return to the beach where the women, children, and old people had been anxiously watching the fighting. Now they joyfully awaited the victors, the saviors of Jagua. The waiting crowd stirred, pointed, and shouted impatiently. The warriors' canoes approached, two by two, towing those of the defeated. The Herculean figure of Ornoya stood out. Arms folded and with the wind in the delicate feathers on his proud head, he watched the rejoicing of his warriors and smiled at the unrestrained celebrations of his people.

Part Two

The Rabbit's Ears

At the start of Creation, Rabbit complained to the Almighty that he had made him very small. While he didn't wish to be as big as Camel or Elephant, he would have liked to be as least as big as Goat and not as tiny as he was, despite having fur and four legs. God replied that he did not wish to set a precedent by modifying his creations but that if Rabbit got him an eagle feather, a lion's tooth, and a serpent's egg, he would make him bigger.

Rabbit made a calabash whistle and blew it on top of the mountain. This made Eagle appear. "How dare you? What are you blowing?"

"It's a hair from my body that sounds once a day so that animals I could eat will come to me. But I eat other food. What I need is one of your feathers so that they will respect me. Give me the feather and I will give you one of my sounding hairs for it."

After the deal was done, Eagle waited for a day and then another and another, but the hair made no sound at all. Meanwhile, Rabbit had got the feather.

The whistling calabash woke Serpent, who came out of the undergrowth and appeared before Rabbit. The deal was done in the same way as with Eagle except that Snake, who in those days still had legs, wanted to have a sounding toenail. This was just as easily done. Rabbit pulled out Snake's toenail and stayed to look after its nest while it recovered from the pain.

A lion coming out of its cave suddenly heard the whistling calabash. He was even more surprised when the Rabbit began to laugh in front of him.

"How dare you? What are you making that noise with?"

"It is a hair from my body that makes this noise once a day so that the animals I would eat if I didn't eat roots, shoots, and fine herbs will come to me. What I need to make them respect me is one of your teeth. You won't need it anymore because the hair alone will bring food to your mouth without any effort."

Everyone wants food to reach their mouths without any effort, and Lion handed over the tooth.

Rabbit arrived before God carrying its load.

"Rabbit! If you can manage to do such things with the size you are, you would be the bane of creation if you were as big as Camel or even Goat! You don't need to be any bigger than you are!"

Rabbit was going on his way very sadly and lurching along when the Almighty, ashamed, called him back and said, pulling his ears: "There, now you have very big ears; but you don't need to be any bigger than you are."

The Cayman's Music

The Cayman played very fine music and he was proud of it. One day, Dog, going to bathe in the river, heard it. "Hey, pal, lend me your music," said Dog.

The Cayman lent him the whistle, and Dog began to play it like this:

> Findicabón, findicabón
> Pito casiba nué,
> Congo na luanga.

This was the music of the whistle.

The Cayman said: "OK, pal, you've had your turn at playing," and he asked him for the music.

"All right, pal, but let me have that pleasure once more," replied the Dog.

The Cayman agreed to let him play it again, but Dog did this: he snatched the whistle, hid it in his mouth, and, when the Cayman least expected it, he made off with it. Dog made a lot of money with the whistle. He played and played:

Findicabón, findicabón
Pito casiba nué,
Congo na luanga.

When asked who the music was by, the Dog replied: "It's not my music; God sent it to me."

When they asked where it came from, he declared: "From Dian-garangón, a very strange place."

The king's daughter died, and they sent for the Dog to play at the funeral. The Dog, who gave himself airs, agreed to play his whistle.

Thus it was that the foolish Cayman lost his music and allowed himself to be tricked.

The Owl's Dance

The Owl was very aloof and did not mix with the other birds. She wished to set herself above them. The Owl was white, and the birds hated her and planned to take revenge for her snubs. But as she did not go out by day, and as she was so aloof, they had no chance of taking their revenge. So they did this: they decided to invite her to a party so that she would be caught by the light of day.

Owl went to the party, and all the birds began to dance and dance and dance.

"Is it day yet?" Owl asked.

"Not yet, far from it!"

And she kept on dancing.

"Is it day yet?"

"Not yet, let the party continue, cachumba, cachumba, cachumba," said the birds so they could catch her out in the light of day.

As soon as daybreak came, the birds said: "We wanted to catch you here," and they pecked and pecked her until her head was doing the cancan.

The Owl promised not to be aloof anymore.

The Tortoise and the Dog

The Tortoise and the Dog lived together and bathed every day in the river. The Tortoise confessed to the Dog that she took the longest baths. While Dog was bathing in the river, Tortoise, who had a secret passage from the river to the house, ate the food, came back, and said to Dog: "Buddy, you don't know how to bathe. I do; I take long baths."

When they arrived home, the Tortoise assured him that it was a thief who was stealing the food. Dog became tired of all this and he went to consult the babalao[1] who ordered him to place a wax doll in the house and wait.

When Tortoise came in and saw the doll, she said: "You came to steal and so have I!" and she hit it. When her little hand stuck to it, she said: "Let go of me! You have come to steal and so did I!" She hit it again, and her other hand stuck fast. As she could not free herself, as soon as Dog returned from bathing in the river, he discovered that Tortoise was the thief. Ever since then they have lived apart.

 # The Tortoise and the Toad

Many years ago, Mrs. Tortoise married one of her daughters to a turtle. She invited all the tortoises, turtles, crabs, lobsters, octopuses, and all the fish to celebrate the marriage. It was a very important wedding, as the little Tortoise who was getting married was a distinguished member of her tribe, and the bridegroom was king of all the turtles.

It so happened that Mother Tortoise, having sent out so many invitations, forgot to invite an old toad, the king of the toads and frogs. Mr. Toad was offended and called together his whole family to decide on a severe punishment for the tortoise who had slighted them. Some said that war should be declared on the tortoises; others that the wedding be stopped by carrying off the bridegroom. Others said that the bride should be killed.

Finally, after much shouting, the old toad said: "The punishment will be even more severe than anything you have suggested. Mrs. Tortoise, who is very proud, has prepared a huge banquet for after the wedding, and I have thought of a way to make a fool of her. While they are in church celebrating the marriage, we will go to the house and eat all the food for the banquet."

And so it was. While they were at church all the frogs and toads arrived at Mrs. Tortoise's house, which was beside the sea. They sat down at the table that was already laid with hams, chickens, cheeses, sweet things, wines, and so on and ate everything up. Many of them got drunk and remained there lying on the floor; others went away. But the old toad hid himself under a stone to await the arrival of the Tortoise, the bride and groom, and the guests.

After a while, the ceremony at the church ended, and the retinue emerged. The young Tortoise went on ahead with the turtle. They were walking very slowly because, whenever they speeded up, Mrs. Tortoise rebuked them so that people would not gossip. Mrs. Tortoise followed behind with a prawn, and behind them came the relatives and guests, who were licking their lips at the mere thought of the food that was waiting for them and that had been so much talked about.

The toad, hidden under a stone, was bursting with satisfaction. He swelled up from time to time and lifted the stone to see if the bride and groom were coming. Finally everyone arrived at the pace of the Tortoise. The youngest of them, being the most indiscreet, began to shout and ask for the food. When Mrs. Tortoise, who at that moment was with an old tortoise, describing the menu to him, heard the guests' angry shouts, she rushed out to see what was happening. She got such a shock when she saw the empty serving dishes that she fainted and hid her head inside her shell.

The guests thought Mrs. Tortoise had deceived them. Although the tortoise and her husband the turtle tried to convince them otherwise, they began to leave, making spiteful comments. A crab from the mangrove swamp who had come with his overweight wife told the angry newlyweds that the marriage had begun with deceit and sham and would end badly. The Octopus spread his tentacles and threatened to smash everything up.

Meanwhile, the Old Toad was laughing from beneath the stone. When everyone left he began to shout: "Miz Tortoise, here I am!"

The Tortoise, who was beginning to recover, heard the toad and began to look for him but couldn't find him. She finally had to ask: "Where're you, Friend Toad?"

She suspected that the toad was to blame for what had happened, and she wanted to catch him and give him a jolly good bite. But the Old Toad realized this, and when she found him and went up to him, he urinated in her eyes. He went out, leaping, to rejoin his folks while the Tortoise stayed there, alone, humiliated and humbled.

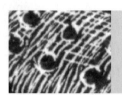

The Monkey
and the Chick Pea

A little monkey bought five cents' worth of chick peas and gave half to her monkey friend, who ate them up and then took one of hers and hid it in his hand.

The little Monkey, weeping, said to him: "Open your hand and give me my chick pea."

"No," said the Monkey.

Then the little Monkey went to the King and said: "King, arrest the monkey so that he will open his hand and give me my chick pea."

"No," replied the King.

The little Monkey went in search of the Queen and said: "Queen, tell the King to catch the monkey so that he will open his hand and give me my chick pea"

"No," said the Queen.

Then the Monkey went in search of the Mouse and said: "Mouse, eat the Queen's clothes so that she will fight with the King if he doesn't arrest the Monkey, so that the Monkey will open his hand and give me my chick pea."

"No," said the Mouse.

She went to the Cat and said: "Cat, eat the Mouse so that the

Mouse will eat the Queen's clothes so that the Queen will fight with the King, so that the King will catch the Monkey and so that the Monkey will open his hand and give me my chick pea."

"No," said the Cat.

The little Monkey went to the Stick and said: "Stick, hit the Cat so that he will eat the Mouse and the Mouse will eat the Queen's clothes so that the Queen will fight with the King, so that the King will catch the Monkey, so that the Monkey will open his hand and give me my chick pea."

"No," answered the Stick.

She went to Fire. "Fire, burn the Stick so that the Stick will hit the Cat, so that he will eat the Mouse and the Mouse will eat the Queen's clothes, so that the Queen will fight with the King, so that the King will catch the Monkey, so that the Monkey will open his hand and give me my chick pea."

"No," said Fire.

She looked for Water and said: "Water, put out the Fire so that the Fire will burn the Stick, so that the Stick will hit the Cat and Cat will eat the Mouse, the Mouse will eat the Queen's clothes, the Queen will fight with the King, so that the King will catch the Monkey, so that the Monkey will open his hand and give me my chick pea."

"No," answered the Water.

The little Monkey went to the Ox and said: "Ox, drink the Water so that Water will put out the Fire, the Fire will burn the Stick, the Stick will hit the Cat, the Cat will eat the Mouse, the Mouse will eat the Queen's clothes, the Queen will fight with the King, so that the King will catch the Monkey and the Monkey will open his hand and give me my chick pea."

"No," said the Ox.

She went to the Ant and said: "Ant, bite the Ox's ass so that the Ox will drink the Water, the Water will put out the Fire, Fire will burn the Stick, the Stick will hit the Cat, the Cat will eat the Mouse, the Mouse will eat the Queen's clothes so that the Queen will fight with the King so that the King will catch the Monkey so that the Monkey will open his hand and give me my chick pea."

"Yes," said the Ant.

"No, I'll drink the water," said the Ox.

"No, I'll put out the Fire," said the Water.

"No, I'll burn the Stick," said the Fire.

"No, I'll hit the Cat," said the Stick.

"No, I'll eat the Mouse," said the Cat.

"No, I'll eat the Queen's clothes," said the Mouse.

"No, I'll fight with the King," said the Queen.

"No, I'll catch the Monkey," said the King.

"No, I'll open my hand and give the bean to the little Monkey," said the

Monkey.

Ambeco and Aguatí

This is the story of Ambeco, which means "deer" in the Carabalí language,[2] and Aguatí, which means "tortoise."

Once upon a time the Deer and the Tortoise came together and made a bet as to which of them could run faster. The bet seemed absurd because the deer can run fast and the tortoise walks very slowly. The Deer laughed at the Tortoise and told him that he was going to win the bet. "I will give you a three-day start!" said the Deer to his opponent.

But the little Tortoise replied: "I don't want any advantage; I just need two weeks to get ready."

They finally agreed on the wager. The winner would be the first to get back to the starting point in town after running down a long road that passed through the two neighboring villages.

The Deer allowed the Tortoise two weeks to get ready, and they went off in different directions, having arranged to meet up on the day of the bet. While the Deer whiled away the time making fun of the Tortoise with all the villagers and other animals, the little Tortoise called on two tortoise friends of hers. She told them that on the day of the bet they should each place themselves in one of the villages through which the race would pass. This was so they could greet the Deer when it arrived and ran alongside them. It would think that it was the same little Tortoise who had made the bet but that appeared to have arrived before him at each of the villages along the route. So it was arranged.

The day of the race came. Each of the Tortoise's friends stationed themselves in one of the two villages, and the little Tortoise joined the Deer in the village to begin the race. The signal was given and they began to run. The Deer soon disappeared from view, and the little Tortoise, instead of running, hid under a bush.

The Deer kept on running, now and then happily singing the following song:

> Ambeco rimagüe quindan-dá, core nyaó
> Ambeco rimagüe quindan-dá, core nyaó
> Ambeco rimagüe quindan-dá, core nyaó

When he reached the first village, the Deer, who in those days had a thick beard like goats today, thinking he had such a head start over the little Tortoise that he had time for a shave, went to find a barber. When he found one, he told him what had happened, saying as before:

> Ambeco rimagüe quindan-dá, core nyaó,
> Ambeco rimagüe quindan-dá, core nyaó,
> Ambeco rimagüe quindan-dá, core nyaó.

But he had barely finished his song and was still only half shaven when he saw a Tortoise on the road who sang to him thus:

> Aguatí langué, langué, langué,

> Aguatí langué, langué, langué,
> Aguatí langué, langué, langué.

This song meant: "The Tortoise has arrived, has arrived, has arrived."

The Deer, when he saw and heard the tortoise, thought that it was the same tortoise he had made the bet with. He gave a start and ran out without finishing his shave. This is why the deer only has hair on one side of his face.

The Deer carried on running, confident of his great speed. He thought that even if he had lost the first part of the contest, he could not lose the second, and he began to sing once more:

> Ambeco rimagüe quindan-dá, core nyaó,
> Ambeco rimagüe quindan-dá, core nyaó,
> Ambeco rimagüe quindan-dá, core nyaó.

In this way he reached the second village and, because he was hungry and thought that he had plenty of time, he went happily to eat. He was so happy that he began to eat and sing:

> Ambeco rimagüe quindan-dá, core nyaó,
> Ambeco rimagüe quindan-dá, core nyaó,
> Ambeco rimagüe quindan-dá, core nyaó.

He had not eaten more than a few mouthfuls, nor finished his song, when he saw a tortoise who sang to him thus:

> Aguatí langué, langué, langué,
> Aguatí langué, langué, langué,

Aguatí langué, langué, langué.

When he heard this the Deer thought that the Tortoise had already arrived. Amazed, he started to run without finishing his meal. This is why, ever since then, the deer is unable to eat much nor in a relaxed manner and has a "very hollow" stomach.

The Deer ran and ran, heading back now toward the village they'd started from, very confident that he would win the bet and arrive before the little Tortoise. And the Deer entered the village singing as before:

Ambeco rimagüe quindan-dá, core nyaó,
Ambeco rimagüe quindan-dá, core nyaó,
Ambeco rimagüe quindan-dá, core nyaó.

But when she heard the Deer entering the village, the little Tortoise, who was hiding under a bush, came out from her hiding place and began to cover the few yards to the finishing line. She got there ahead of the deer and began to sing:

Aguatí langué, langué, langué,
Aguatí langué, langué, langué,
Aguatí langué, langué, langué.

When the Deer arrived and saw that the Tortoise had got there first, he was furious. The whole village and all the other animals made fun of him because he had lost the bet. The Deer was so ashamed that he fled into the mountains, never wishing to return to the village. This is why nowadays the deer stays shyly in the forest and will only be drawn out by force.

The Pitirre
and the Cotunto[3]

Once upon a time the Pitirre and the Cotunto were debating whether it was more effective and advantageous to be cunning or to be honest and trustworthy. The Cotunto, very put out, declared that in certain circumstances cunning and guile were no use at all. The Pitirre maintained that, at the most difficult times, one needed a little cunning and guile, intelligence and prudence in order to succeed. And they debated at length, without seeing the other's point of view, because that is how it always is.

As neither of the sorry creatures would give in, they made a bet. Each of them would perch on the branch of a tree. The conditions were clearly specified: they were not to sleep or move from it, not even to eat or drink. They then positioned themselves in such a way that, if either flew away, the other would notice and he would lose the bet. From time to time one or other of them had to sing to show that they were awake. Once the bet was agreed, it fell to the Cotunto to sing first. He sang this song in a hoarse, tuneless voice:

> Cofina güe, ananá
> Aú, aú, ananá
> Cofina güe.

As soon as the Cotunto finished, the Pitirre responded in a shrill and piercing voice:

> Cofina güe, ananá
> Aú, aú, ananá
> Cofina güe.

They carried on like this throughout the evening and into the night without eating or sleeping. At daybreak, they felt so weak that they could not go on much longer. They sang in faint voices and could barely be heard. The Pitirre, true to his principles, looked for a way of winning by using his cunning. He was thinking this over when he saw a butterfly approaching and, zap! without thinking, he ate it.

As he had managed not to move from his perch, the honest Cotunto suspected nothing, although he was surprised that when the Pitirre sang:

> Cofina güe, ananá
> Aú, aú, ananá
> Cofina güe.

He was singing in a more lively fashion.

When the Cotunto sang again he tried to copy the Pitirre, but he only managed to make himself weaker, and he lost all his resolve.

The Pitirre repeated his song, but this time he waited in vain for the Cotunto's response as, by playing fair in the wager, he died of hunger, exhaustion, and thirst.

The Pitirre gathered together his brothers, and they agreed to always use cunning to triumph under difficult circumstances.

From then on, the Cotunto would be obliged to retreat whenever the victorious Pitirre appeared, and they sang their hymn of victory in unison

> Cofina güe, ananá
> Aú, aú, ananá
> Cofina güe.

The Owl and the Monkey

At the time of this legend, the Owl was able to see by day and by night, and the Monkey could speak fluently, matching words to his gestures. They enjoyed a deep and sincere friendship. At that time, the Owl was known to be intelligent and trustworthy, for which outstanding virtues Day showered him with attention. Over time he became his close confidant.

On one occasion, Day asked the Owl to help him to divest the Moon of her symbols so that she would be obliged to serve him. It is important to point out that Day was friendly with all the stars but not with the Moon, who was not only extremely unsociable but also vain and conceited.

The Day ordered the Owl to send a message inviting the Moon to a lavish feast. To do this he used ink with magical powers. It would blind her when she read the message. In order to present her with the invitation, the Owl had to wear a cloak that would protect him from witchcraft.

As soon as he had written the message, the Owl went to meet the Moon. On the long journey he met his dear friend Monkey, whom he told in detail about the Day's plans, not realizing they were being watched by the dark Vulture, who was hidden in a nearby tree. Seizing his chance, the Vulture flew off and told the Moon what the Monkey and the Owl had been talking about.

When the Moon heard this, she took the necessary precautions for warding off the witchcraft, and hurling all her power into space, she caused a state of total darkness that produced the first eclipse. The Day, who had been watching all the actions of the proud Moon, realized her allies were careless and foolish, and he ordered them to appear before him.

After scolding them for their behavior, he forced the Owl, who tried hard to avoid the punishment, to read the message that was intended for the Moon. It made him blind, a victim of the witchcraft. When he saw his friend Owl's plight, the Monkey began to cry out in terror. The Day took advantage of this to make the Monkey keep his mouth open and drink a certain potion that silenced him forever.

Because they had been indiscreet and talkative, the Owl would never again see the light of day, and the Monkey lost the gift of speech.

Siquillángama

The story begins with this typical song that is also a dance. It is used to begin many other stories:

(This means: "Listen carefully, for I'm about to tell you something extraordinary.")

When Gren-Dami, the village chief, died, his son Ecue-Ibonó became the head of the family. He married twenty wives to form his family. The senior wife ruled over all the others. Her name was Maurú. Since then, all the powerful men in Africa have many wives. When one wife becomes pregnant, some young man will take on the duty of raising the infant if it is a boy; if it is a girl he takes her as his wife.

Maurú and Ecue-Ibonó's other wives, like all the women there, spent their time fishing, farming, and taking care of the house. Their husband was a warrior and a hunter, like all the worthy men of his land. He spent seasons far away in the bush, hunting. When he returned, his wives welcomed him with feasting, drumming, and dancing.

Close by the house was a great river that flowed into the sea. The women used to fish in it. One time when Ecue-Ibonó returned from the hunt and they had found a lot of fish to eat, he called Maurú and warned her not to catch a large fish called Siquillángama, which has little bells on its gills, because he is the king of the river.

Maurú promised, but as soon as he went back to the bush, she called all the women, and they went to the river to catch the big fish with little bells on its gills. They entered the water with the fish trap and freeing the little fish that fell in, set out to catch the big one. Siquillángama fell into the trap and began to sing:

Siguillángama in the river

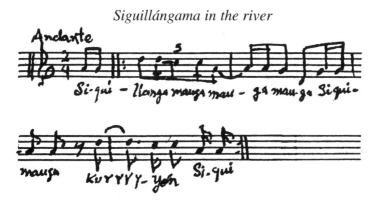

Thus he sang, and then he escaped. ("Kurr" is the sound of the fish scraping against the trap, and "Yón" is the sound of him falling into the water as he escaped.)

They managed to trap him in one of these, and they served him to their husband at the first feast they gave on his return from the bush. The head with its gills was thrown into the loft in the hut so as to hide it. Everyone was at table, but no one could have anything to eat until Ecue-Ibonó had started, as he was the man and the head of the family. He called for soup, and when he dipped his calabash ladle in the copper pot, he served himself a nice piece of fish along with the soup. But when he tasted it, everyone could hear singing coming from the loft. It was Siquillgama's head, which sang:

Siquillángama in the loft

(This means: "I am the man of the river whom you told them not to catch.")

("Pacá, pacá" is the sound of the quills flapping against the poles of the loft.)

Ecue-Ibonó and all the others began to dance to the rhythm of the song, and they kept on dancing without having a bite to eat until they fell down exhausted and weary that night. The following day, when they tried to have lunch, the singing and dancing began again, but this time it went on for three days and nights.

(At this point storyteller and listeners start singing and dancing again for as long as they please.)

The wives, understanding the problem, decided to offer Ecue-bonó another dish, rice, to distract his attention from the fish that would not allow itself to be eaten and that had exhausted them all with its singing.

No sooner said than done. They began to pound rice on those large wooden African mortars with pestles over a meter long. They sing and dance to this song, miming the pounding of the grain:

The song of the pestle

(This means: "Put water on to heat as the rice is being ground.")

Then they winnowed the straw to the beat of another merry song performed while they mime the action of sieving the grain and throwing the straw in the air.

The song of the sieve

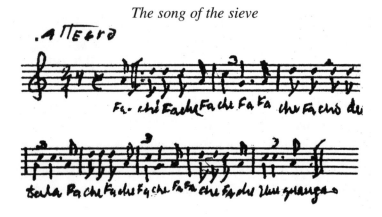

("Faché, faché" is the sound of the rice on the bottom and sides of the sieve.)

They served him the rice, but Ecue-Ibonó wanted to start with the soup as usual. When he tasted the fish, the head in the loft began to sing, as before. He asked them what fish they had served him, and his second wife told him how, against her husband's wishes, Maurú had caught Siquillánama, the lord of the river.

The husband asked for the head and saw that it really did have little bells on its gills. He called all his wives and made them throw the head into the river, and then he sent them all away.

Siquillánama revived and began to swim, singing:

Siquillángama in the river

Since then men have never trusted women.

The Black Man
Who Felled a Ceiba Tree

Once upon a time there was a black man who used to go through a meadow where a goat was eating grass. On the first day when he saw the goat, the black man, who was very stubborn, said: "Hmm! You eatin' grass right where people passin' by."

The next day he said the same thing and threatened to pull one of its horns out if it stayed there. And as he passed through the meadow every day saying to the goat, "You eatin' grass where people passin' by," the poor animal took fright and was so upset that it gave the black man a horn.

The black man then went to the sea and offered to give him the goat's horn in exchange for a little fish. At first the sea did not want to do the deal, but the black man visited him every day and pestered him until he made the sea so sick that it gave him a little fish in exchange for the horn.

When the black man had the fish he went to the house of a blacksmith to get fire to cook the fish that the sea had given him in exchange for the goat's horn. He went every day to ask the smith for fire and told him the tale of what had happened to him and why he wanted the fire, until the smith got fed up and gave him fire.

The black man went to his house and cooked the fish that the sea had given him in exchange for the horn that the goat had given him on the fire that the smith had given him. But as he was cooking the little fish he set his arm on fire and ran out. As he was passing another smithy, the smith took the fire from his arm and told him he had done this because he needed it.

The black man complained that he had taken away the fire that the other smith had given him to cook the fish the sea had given him in exchange for the horn the goat had given him. And after he had gone to the forge for many days with the same tiresome refrain, the smith gave him a hammer.

The black man went away very pleased with his hammer, but, as he was passing another forge, the smith took the hammer off him because he needed it, even though the black man told him that another smith had given him the hammer in exchange for the fire that he had taken from his arm, that he had for cooking the fish that the sea had given him in exchange for the horn the goat gave him. And as he told the same story every day, the smith, extremely bored, gave him the hatchet from his workshop in exchange.

The black man was very happy with the axe because he believed that he would make himself rich with it. He went into the forest to cut down trees. But as he was very stupid and had never done this type of work, he struck the first ceiba[4] tree he found with his axe, and when he cut the trunk it fell on him and crushed him. This is why, ever since then, blacks do not cut down ceiba trees.

The River

The hordes of men advanced deep into the impenetrable forest, savagely tearing down the dense trees, trampling the green grass that grew on the paths and pulling up by the roots the slender bushes that blocked their destructive impulse. They built roads. Narrow paths carpeted with fallen leaves appeared that gave way to wide roads skirting the high and inaccessible mountains that rose to meet their natural ceiling: the sky.

In this way man created his communication routes and extended the boundaries of the villages, establishing new links and taking possession of more and more of the forest's jealously guarded secrets. In the wildest and densest part of the forest where the harshness of the terrain curbed man's audacity, the river flowed, majestic and menacing. From the highest plateaus it could be seen meandering through the mountains like a silvery monster that moves forward sluggishly. But when the distance was covered in a determined effort, the river, seen from nearby, revealed all its fury, its choppy water, its raging eddies rising, writhing like a wounded serpent rippling its back in the throes of death. The river roared lugubriously, a thunderous and menacing sound. Even the bravest hearts were filled with awe, and no one dared risk the dangerous undertaking of conquering the current.

When all the others had left, convinced that any attempt to conquer the river would be fruitless, Agallú Solá, a farmer who was elderly but as strong and vigorous as a young warrior and irascible and hardworking, stood beside it looking at it defiantly. After thinking for a moment, he took his sharp axe and began to cut down a huge tree. Its trunk was so wide that it could not comfortably be encircled by the arms of five people. When he had finally felled it, he stripped away the branches with his battle machete. He made a bonfire whose sputtering flames rose, illuminating the sky with its bright sparks.

Then he let a slow fire bore through the resinous trunk of the felled tree while he shaped the wood until he had fashioned a crude boat. He made two powerful oars out of the same wood. When he considered his work done, he put some provisions in his boat and set out on his adventure. He rowed, cutting through the current, beating it tirelessly with his oars. The river put up a resistance equal to that of a thousand animals pulling in the same direction. But Agallú Solá cut through the river in his small boat. All his muscles flexed, and the veins on his neck stood out, his chest expanding and contracting like an accordion. The oars hit the water, *thwack, thwack, thwack.* The river raged furiously, *rrr rrr.* Rocking wildly, the boat moved forward. Agallú inched forward. Every inch gained was one less opportunity for the river to swallow him and his boat. The daring boatman rowed more swiftly though the current that gradually became less strong.

Once he had covered half the distance, Agallú gathered strength and, with odd movements, he broke through the current, making the boat move forward rapidly until it reached the opposite bank of the river. He leaped ashore and, rubbing his hands together, said: "I have conquered you; now I will finish you off."

Without pausing for breath, he climbed into the boat again and crossed the river, this time with much less effort than in the first contest.

Agallú Solá did this ten times until he turned the river into a calm, quiet stream on which the boat glided slowly and smoothly. Thanks to Agallú's efforts, contact was established between the villages that had the river as their boundary. In return for his achievement, anyone who wanted to cross over to the other side had to pay a fee to the farmer who had become a boatman. He also became a wealthy man.

One day a woman arrived on the riverbank. Dressed in a voluminous coarse woollen cloth, she had a beautiful face and good manners. She climbed into the boat, indicating to the boatman that he should take her to the other side. When he saw her distinguished appearance, Agallú thought it prudent not to mention the fee for his work. Settling her comfortably in his boat, he began to row. When they reached the bank, the woman jumped up and began patiently arranging the folds of her skirt, scarcely looking at the boatman. This gave Agallú an opportunity to claim his payment. "Omordé,[5] pay me the fee."

The woman responded by taking off her dress and lying down on the grass. Agallú, seeing her thus, mounted her, and they had sexual intercourse. Afterwards the woman said: "You have had the great honor of sleeping with Obatalá." And she disappeared, leaving the boatman bewildered.

And that was that.

Aché[6]

Without knowing it, Agayu Solá had possessed Obatalá, the most powerful woman among those lares, who had the gift of being able to transform her appearance. Sometimes she appeared in the guise of a humble and gentle lover, sometimes in that of a warrior full of fighting spirit, able to perform valiant deeds, giving orders arrogantly, and treating her enemies ruthlessly. But this one adventure had not satisfied the ferryman. He felt his manhood humiliated. He needed to find out who Obatalá was. He thought that the most proper thing would have been for him to make the first move as men usually do. That is why he changed his manner toward those who came to cross the river. To each one that came he said: "Who are you and where do you come from?"

And they had to answer: "I am so-and-so."

"Well, pay me the fee."

"Here it is."

If this procedure was not followed, Agallú Solá would fold his arms and remain deaf to all requests. When anyone insisted he would say: "Find a name and a coin and you may cross the river; otherwise you are just a miserable timewaster."

Lo and behold one day a child appears before him and says:

"Agayu Solá, I want to go and see my mother who is on the other side."

"What is your name, moquenquen?"[7]

"I don't have a name."

"Well, in that case I can't help you."

The child began to cry and retorted: "It's been a long time since I saw my iyare;[8] perhaps after this I may never see her again. Take me."

"How many coins do you have?"

"I am very poor."

Then the ferryman answered: "Moquenquen, go back to where you came from. I cannot violate my principles."

"Then carry me on your shoulders. You have never said 'I will charge you so much for carrying you on my shoulders.'"

"You are smart; I will carry you," said Agallú, lifting the child and entering the river. But as soon as he began to walk he noticed that the child grew heavier and heavier until he was an unbearable weight. "What the hell is making you so heavy?" Agallú asked him, struggling to keep him on his shoulder.

"Don't ask questions, and keep your word."

"Moquenquen, I can't go on."

"Then look at me!"

The ferryman turned his face toward the child and cried out, letting him fall into the water. "Odu-dua!"

The child, floating on the water, came up to him and said: "For your efforts, I hand the river over to you."

Then he disappeared. And that was that.

Punishment

After her meeting with Agallú Solá, Obatalá assumed the avatar of Osan-quiriñán[9] and climbed the peaks leading to her snowy white ilé.[10] There she devoted herself to her duties, not attaching any importance to her fleeting adventure. Soon afterward she felt the discomfort that precedes motherhood. But the woman did not worry, and she continued to be absorbed in her tasks. Until one day she felt very intense pains, as if something was trying to escape from her insides.

Obatalá said: "I will push until it comes out."

Soon after, a child emerged. The woman who had just given birth took him in her arms and stroking him, said: "You will be called Changó."

"I like that name," said the moquenquen.

After this, Obatalá returned to her affairs and did not take any notice of the moquenquen. He got bored and ran from one end of the house to the other, or he remained lying on the floor, his eyes fixed on the dome of sky for long stretches of time. When he saw his mother coming, he clutched at her, hugging her legs, and asked with tears in his eyes: "Obatalá, who is my father?"

"I don't know, moquenquen; don't pester me!"

Changó wept. "Waah, waah, waah . . ." And he detached himself from his mother, dragging his little legs along the ground, very
distressed and sad.

On the following day he said to his mother again: "Obatalá, I
want to see my father!"

"Moquenquen, I don't have time to answer you."

And every day it was the same: "My iyare, I want to see my
father!"

Until one day Obatalá, fed up, replied: "It's Agallú Solá; go
and stay with him!" She had barely finished her sentence when
Changó swiftly escaped, sliding down the mountains like a gazelle. He disappeared into the forest, shouting: "Agallú Solá!
Agallú Solá!"

It so happened that Agallú Solá still remembered the woman.
He thought about her every afternoon, and he would go into the
forest, stricken with an inexplicable rage. He walked so quickly
that he left trees swaying in his wake. He wept copious tears that
beat heavily on the dry leaves scattered on the ground. And the forest was filled with sadness. The afternoons went by slowly and
monotonously, for Agallú Solá was so affected by the memory of
the woman that he lost all sense of time.

That afternoon he heard the child's voice calling out his name,
and he stopped in the bend of a path to wait for him.

"What are you looking for, moquenquen?"

"I'm looking for my father."

"And you, who are you?"

"I'm Babá's[11] child."

When he heard this, Agallú trembled with rage and asked him
again: "Who is your father?"

"You are."

Then Agallú said: "Moquenquen, I am far too hungry to listen to all your nonsense. I will roast you, and you will do me for a meal."

Changó did not turn a hair and said to him, smiling: "You will not kill me; you are my father."

"No? Wait and see."

Agallú took some branches, piled them up, and set them alight. He began to stoke up the fire in front of the impassive boy, who had not stopped smiling. When the bonfire was burning brightly, he took the boy by the arms and threw him onto it. He said, laughing to himself, "Today I will feed on your tender flesh."

The fire hissed and threw a thousand sparks into the air that lit up the fading afternoon with their faint glow. The many-tongued flames licked harmlessly at the body of the child, who stood proudly in the middle of the blaze.

"Oh, moquenquen, now you'll be fried to a crisp," said Agallú, and, taking a branch, he hit him brutally. An omordé was passing. When she saw the child's plight, she ran until she reached the next village and shouted out news of Agallú Solá's crime. The people rose up and began to give their views. Some said: "We should go there and punish Agallú." Others said: "The most sensible thing would be to inform Olofi."

Two women, Oyá and Ochún, agreed to take the news to Olofi after it was decided that his authority must be relied upon to resolve any untoward behavior.

When Olofi was informed of the matter, he said to Oyá, handing her a flash of lightning: "Go and light up the forest. The rest is done." Turning to the other woman, he said: "Bring me the child."

When Agallú Solá saw the flash of lightning approaching, he ran away, terrified, bounding like an ape. He stopped in front of a palm tree and climbed it in a trice. He stayed there, trembling with fear.

Ochún rescued the moquenquen from the flames, and both women returned to Olofi. Olofi said, referring to Changó: "I will make you lord of the fire!"

To Oyá he said: "You are the mistress of lightning!"

Turning to Ochún, he said: "It will be your turn another day. I have handed out a lot of aché today."

And that was that.

Destiny

Changó returned home happy. His wish to see his father had been granted. That was enough for him, despite the harsh reception. In his innocence, he did not know how fathers were supposed to behave toward their children, and therefore his own reception had seemed right and proper. As soon as he arrived, he went to Obatalá and said: "My iyare, I have been with my father."

Obatalá laughed her head off, showing her white teeth. "You won't want to see him again."

"On the contrary, Babá: he gave me a very pleasant day."

"Really? Why didn't you stay with him?"

"I wanted to come and give you the news. Besides, he taught me many things: look." The boy went over to the oven and takes out a burning coal. He passed it over his body and then chewed it, licking his lips as if it were a sweet.

Obatalá said to him: "I see that you can eat fire. Who gave you this gift?"

"My father!"

"Moquenquen, you are lying!"

"I'm telling the truth; my father took me before Olofi and said to him: 'Give my son a gift,' and God replied: 'He will be the lord of fire.'"

"What your father has taught you is the gift of lying!"

"Oh, I see that you hate my father."

"Child, you are a lying skirtchaser." Then she seized him and began to smack him hard on the backside until her hands swelled up. The child struggled to free himself, but Obatalá held him between her legs and hit him even more determinedly, saying: "This is so that you never speak to me of your father again."

"Waah, waah, waah," cried Changó.

Obatalá hit him until she fell down exhausted and Changó was swollen and shapeless like a lump of meat.

From then on Changó kept out of Obatalá's way. His spirit was overcome with resentment, and the formerly melancholy child became a boisterous, alarming creature who disturbed the legendary peace of Obatalá's home. He ran from place to place, tirelessly dragging any objects he found along the ground, ringing the ritual handbells. That was some of the time; other times, no sooner had he got out of bed than he began to snoop in all the corners, finding Obatalá's secret objects and throwing them onto the floor with a scornful gesture. His mother punished him severely. When he had taken his punishment he ran over the mountains and turned up at the güemilere. He learned how to dance alongside the drums like the professional dancers, and he gained the affection of those present.

When he arrived they would say: "It is the child that Agallú tried to burn." And the drummers let him beat play the drum used at the party with his restless fingers. Changó drank glasses of liquor and in a drunken and euphoric state returned to his habit of grabbing everything.

One day he found an amulet carefully wrapped in soft cotton

balls, and, seeing it was very nice, he said: "Do you want to have fun at the güemilere?"

The amulet answered: "As long as you put me back in my place afterward."

They arrived at the party arm-in-arm, like two pals. As soon as the gris-gris heard the music, it jumped up and down three times and danced to the beat. Changó danced with him, following his steps.

Then they said: "Let's have a drink!"

"Well, let's then!"

They drank quickly until they had their fill, and they partied on more wildly, letting the days go by, unmindful of Obatalá and of everyone else. On the sixth day, the güemilere drew to a close with a song to Elegúa, and they went home together completely drunk.

When she saw them, Obatalá said to Changó: "Damn! Didn't you know that Odú-dua must not see daylight?"

"But he's had a good time," answered Changó.

Obatalá, furious, seized him and, holding him up in the air, let him fall rapidly into space, saying: "You are trying to wreck my house; but I'll bury you in the ground first."

Here began the heroic deeds of Changó de Ima.

The Revelation

A villager called Yemayá was busy with her household chores when the heavens suddenly clouded over and it began to thunder loudly as if the sky was threatening to shatter into a thousand pieces. The noise of the furious march of the thunder was like the unrestrained gallop of an enormous cavalcade. The advancing clouds cautiously unraveled their curly fleece, moving sluggishly and hiding the last traces of a reddened sun.

Suddenly a flash of lightning cut through space, hurting the eyes of the omordé, who looked up instinctively and was surprised to see a red dot falling rapidly toward her.

Not batting an eyelid, Yemayá opened her skirt out like an net and waited for the incandescent sphere to fall. It shattered in a thick cloud of smoke and threw her to the ground, startling her. After a moment, the woman was even more amazed when she saw before her a child, who was gazing at her and smiling.

"Moquenquen, who are you?" asked the astonished Yemayá.

"I am Changó; my mother has thrown me out of heaven."

"And who is your iyare?"

"Obatalá."

Then Yemayá said happily: "Oh, Changó, you are a gift that

Olofi has deigned to send me. I will raise you with care."

Then she took him to her house. First she gave him a beautiful pair of shoes.

"Nice achó,"[12] said the child, putting them on.

Then she gave him clothes. The child threw them away, saying to the woman: "I don't want batá;[13] the best thing you can do is take me to the güemilere."

"I am here to do your bidding, she replied. And, taking him by the hand, she presented him to the drums, and they danced around them until the party drew to a close.

They went back to the house, where no sooner did Changó arrive than he began to scream: "Give me my amalá,[14] miserable woman!"

Yemayá immediately prepared a meal for him, and Changó ate sumptuously. When he was full he demanded: "Now I want to sleep on a mat that is not as dirty as yours."

"Very well, my iyá,"[15] answered Yemayá, giving him a richly woven one.

As soon as the boy lay down he fell fast asleep. The omordé slept beside him. But soon afterward Changó opened his eyes and began to kick Yemayá on the behind. "Lazybones, serve your son," he said to her.

Yemayá patiently asked him: "What do you want, my iyá?"

"Find me some drums at once to entertain me," he answered. Yemayá brought him drums decorated with bright red ribbons. Changó took them and spent the whole night playing them and singing:

> Oh, baricosó
> Baricosó,

Baricosó,
Alardemí oooh!
Alardosó, cabo!
Alardosó, cabo!
Alardemí, oooh!

Roused by the music, Yemayá got up from her seat and began
to dance, singing in accompaniment to the child who, seeing her
enthusiasm, angrily pushed aside the drums, saying: "My maid,
you may not dance, the best thing is for you to take care of me. Go
to the forest and bring me some oguedé."[16]

The omordé had to go a long way to indulge him. Taking a sack,
she set off and went deep into the forest.

After a while Changó lit a fire and made the ilé go up in flames.
Then he went inside and settled down on his mat as if nothing had
happened.

From afar, Yemayá saw the sudden blaze and, without having
got the bananas, ran to her son's aid. Unable to extinguish the fire,
she put her hands on her head and cried: "Olofi, don't let the
moquenquen be burned to a cinder."

And as the flames crackle more furiously, Changó appeared
from among them and, standing before the woman, said: "I wanted to test you. Where are the oguedé? Coward!"

"How was I to bring them if I thought you were burning?"

"Oh, I can see you're completely useless. I'm leaving," said
Changó.

"No, don't do that. Why don't you ask me to do the most difficult thing I can for you, moquenquen," Yemayá said to him
humbly.

"Then find me the ekuelé divining tray that Obatalá hides

in her ilé."

The woman, even though she knew how difficult her task was, told the child that she would perform it. She set off on an arduous journey, walking without resting, climbing steep ridges and peaks of sharp rock that covered her hands and feet in wounds, turning them into a misshapen mass. But Yemayá gathered together all her strength and continued her trek. With a huge effort, she reached Obatalá's door and fell down weakly before her, bleeding all over and half dead.

She remained unconscious for a long time. When she came around she was very ashamed when she saw before her Changó, holding the divining tray in his hands and with not a scratch on his body.

He said to her: "See how lazy you are and as slow as an elephant? You took so long to carry out the errand that I decided to come myself. Now I'm leaving."

Yemayá did not even have the heart to answer, nor to plead with him; she was so exhausted that she stayed in Obatalá's doorway, watching Changó fly swiftly over the sharp, prominent peaks of the path of Osan-quiriñán, the only one leading to the house perched on the inaccessible plateau. Then, worn out, she bowed her head and remained there. She stayed like that for a long time until dusk, when Obatalá arrived, wearing all Olofi's attributes. When she saw Yemayá, she rebuked her: "Yalocha,[17] what are you doing in my doorway?"

The woman said to her: "I came to steal the ekuelé divining tray for Changó, but he has beaten me to it, and after he stole it he left me lying here helpless and without the comfort of having him by my side."

"All right, well, now you will remain in my house for forty days and be my servant. That is your punishment for trying to help Changó."

From that day on Obatalá woke Yemayá each morning with the lash and made her perform the most grueling tasks, always reminding her that: "This is so that you won't meddle in my affairs another day!"

On the fortieth day she let her go and put a little necklace into her hands, saying: "This is the ekuelé[18] chain. Find Changó and give it to him in my name. You will be doing him a great favor."

This time she descended without mishap. When she reached her house she found Changó waiting for her with the divining tray on his legs. He demanded that she hand over the chain. As soon as he took it in his hands, he threw it onto the smooth surface of the divining tray and, according to the different positions in which the necklace fell, described to Yemayá the things that had happened to her and gave her rituals for solving her problems.

Yemayá, amazed, said: "Oh, now I understand why I could not raise you: you are the thrower of the ekuelé."

And that was that.

Forgetfulness

When Changó had grown tired of his hurried and itinerant lifestyle, he installed himself peacefully in a house near to where Yemayá lived. He passed the time giving consultations to the villagers with his divining chain. So successful was he at finding out and getting to the bottom of their problems that he was continually consulted by people whose lives depended on the changing positions of his little chain. He acquired the reputation of a great and prestigious diviner and had so much work that he scarcely had time to develop his other faculties.

The day came when, tired of his profession and eager to return to the life of the güemilere, where the drums awaited the touch of his skillful hands, he decided to abandon the ekuelé. He called Orúmbila, a meticulous and contrary old man, and, handing the divining tray and chain over to him, said: "As I'm bored with my job, I have decided to nominate you my replacement."

"Thank you very much," said Orúmbila. "I will honor you as is right and proper."

"But wait," said Changó. "I should give you some advice. You must use your earnings to look after my friend Elegúa."

"How shall I do that?"

"Well, you have to give him a share of the money each time you divine for an aleyo."[19]

"Very well, I will honor your word generously," said Orúmbila. And he began to throw the chain with consummate wisdom and skill. The rumor soon spread that people were praising his exquisite tact and wonderful capacity for helping everyone who turned up with some insoluble problem. However, every night Elegúa arrived at his door to claim his share. But the old man ignored his obligation.

Elegúa complained: "I have come to collect what is mine."

Orúmbila answered: "We'll settle accounts tomorrow."

Elegúa went away without saying a word. The next day he received a similar answer: "It'll be tomorrow; I haven't had time to settle with you today."

Elegúa waited impassively until one day, without saying anything to Orúmbila, he sat down beside his door at the start of the day and waited until those who wanted answers from the ekuelé came rushing to see the diviner. To each one that came he said: "Orúmbila is not seeing anyone today. He is tired." And to others he said: "The old man has taken the day off to visit his wife."

However, at night he turned up as usual to claim his share. "Will you let me have something?" he pleaded.

Orúmbila, completely bankrupt, answered him angrily: "I haven't earned a penny today. Don't bother me!"

And on the days that followed: "You'd better get lost, you lazy dog!"

But Elegúa ignored his insults and went away. Each morning he went back to keep people away. He sat patiently in Orúmbila's doorway, making everyone go away, extremely disillusioned. And gradually their mistrust of the old man grew as word of his unreliability began to spread. "Changó did the wrong thing when he handed the ekuelé over to that dreadful old man."

And Elegúa, realizing that Orúmbila could not survive much longer, appeared before him one morning. He found him lying downcast and feeble on his mat. He had lost all his nerve, and his jaw was drooping.

"Oh, Orúmbila, what a state you're in! Have you lost the gift of throwing the ekuelé?"

"No, it's not that; it's that the aleyos are not coming."

"And why don't you consult for yourself?"

"I've done that and I didn't get anything."

"Oh, then you have lost the ability! Call Changó."

When he heard this, Orúmbila recovered what strength he had and said to him uneasily: "What does Changó know about this! I'm the only one who knows how to divine with the ekuelé!"

"Very well," said Elegúa, and he went away. He went back a few days later and found him weak, listless, and unkempt, lying miserably on the floor.

"Orula, shall I call Changó?" he asked slyly.

"Call him," the old man answered in a weak voice.

Changó soon appeared. He entered like a warrior, hitting the ground with his steel sword, wearing a brilliant red jacket. He looked haughtily at the old man. Taking the chain, he toyed with it for a moment, then, giving it a swing, threw it uninterestedly onto the divining tray that was lying on the table covered in powder.

"Cheer up, old man, and tell me what the divining chain has to say," he admonished Orúmbila, who attempted to oblige him.

"I lost the ability a few days ago," Orula confessed.

"Oh, then pay my friend what you owe him, and don't bother me with such a trifling matter," said Changó, and he went away.

Orúmbila murmured: "The master knows best." And he did his duty by Elegúa.

That is why, before performing any magical work, it is necessary to give an initial share to Elegúa.

And that was that.

Covetousness

Orúmbila continued to throw the ekuelé. He managed to amass a huge fortune. He need only consider that his daily takings amounted to that of a hundred well-paid workers and that, even if he squandered the money and honored his agreement with Elegúa very generously, he had cash enough to rival the most affluent men of his time. But the old man was thrifty and had simple habits. He took greater pleasure in piling up his earnings, foreseeing some turn of fortune beyond the range of his faculties as a diviner.

Elegúa, who visited him regularly to collect his fee, never imagined that the old man, simply by looking at a divining chain and sorting out the daily difficulties of his fellow men, could have amassed so much profit. In order to fund his ambitions, he began to devise a way of going into partnership with Orúmbila and sharing his earnings.

"How shall I approach this miserly old man and suggest he should share his profits?" he said to himself each day, scratching his head. But no honorable idea came to mind. One day, he found an easy solution to his problems. Snapping his fingers exuberantly, he appeared unexpectedly before his benefactor.

"Orúmbila," he said, emptying a hundred coins onto the divining tray, "I have decided to become your partner. From now on we will share the earnings. I will save you the trouble of reducing your savings by giving me part of them, simply because Changó advised it."

Orúmbila replied: "That is a paltry sum. Besides, I had not thought of sharing my earnings, much less with a beggar like you."

"That's all right," replied Elegúa, and he left, disappearing into the forest. After walking aimlessly for a long time, he stopped in the middle of a vast plain. Uttering some inaudible words, he turned himself into three different beings. Beginning thus his magical work, he said to the first Elegúa: "You will remain in the savannah. Your task is to defame Orula."

And he went away, accompanied by the second Elegúa. He stopped in front of the old man's door, saying: "You will station yourself here and send the aleyos to the house across the road." And he installed himself in the said house with the divining tray and chain, and waited.

When the new day dawned, the aleyos took to the road as usual in a long line that led to the diviner's ilé. But when they reached the vast plain they came upon the solitary inhabitant of the savannah. He inquired: "Where are you off to so early in the morning?"

"We are going to consult Orúmbila," they replied.

"Well, then turn back because the old man has stopped being miserly. He is frittering away the money that he steals from you on women at the güemilere."

The aleyos reply: "We don't doubt your word, but we will see for ourselves."

And the convoy continued marching across the plain. When the first ones arrived, the Elegúa in the doorway went to meet them. He says: "The babalawo has had to go out unexpectedly, and he has advised me to send you to his stand-in at the house across the road."

"Is it true," they ask, "that Orúmbila is squandering the money that we pay him?"

"Oh no! Don't believe the rumors spread by a slanderer," answered the second Elegúa.

And the aleyos, completely trusting, visited in turn the other one who was waiting inside the ilé. He attended them carefully and used the answers of his divining chain to wisely settle their quarrels with false destiny. Each person gladly payed the fee for his visit.

In the days that followed, things happened in the same way; the Elegúa in the doorway always contradicting the one in the savannah. "Don't take any notice of the rumors spread by that jealous person who is trying to hide Orúmbila's merits. He has gone on a long journey: consult his stand-in."

The people eagerly consulted the usurper. With time Orúmbila's reputation gradually declined, and Elegúa's prestige grew. When his magical work had the desired effect, he turned up, prosperous and arrogant, before the real and only thrower of the ekuele. When he saw him dejected and depressed, he said in an affected manner: "Oh, obiní,[20] what is happening to you?"

Orúmbila weakly answered: "My friend, I have had bad luck since you went away. Do you think Changó could resolve this matter?"

"I don't think so," Elegúa answered coldly.

"Call Changó, and I will do what he tells me to," begged the old man.

"No, I would rather see you die."

"At least give me a plate of food as I've already eaten all my savings."

"Die, proud dog; a man of your class shouldn't beg."

Orúmbila said resignedly, "If I must die then let me die. But who will throw the ekuelé?"

"Who better than I, who have managed to steal your clients," replied Elegúa. And, taking him by the shoulders, he pressed him against the wall, then threw him to the ground and hurled a sack of coins at his feet, saying: "This is so that you can recover. To-morrow you will throw the ekuelé according to the deal with your new partner."

The old man bowed his head and whispered: "You are extreme-ly shrewd. I accept your proposal." And the deal was closed.

Hereby end the incidents relating to the ekuelé.

Echú and the Pumpkin

Ochún had a vegetable garden sown with such lovely big pumpkins that there was scarcely room to walk in it comfortably. With Ochún's care and skill, the pumpkins grew fine and abundant. She put a great deal of effort into cultivating them and gave them the best part of her free time. Moreover, she treated them all equally, and the pumpkins were happy to have such a good, hardworking mistress.

On one occasion, a pumpkin began to grow and became so unusually beautiful that it stood out from all the rest. Ochún, seeing it so fine, was captivated by it and began to treat it differently from the others. She paid them less attention. Realizing that their new neighbor had captured the affection of their mistress, they began to be filled with jealousy and agreed to plot against the upstart.

One night they stealthily approached the pumpkin who enjoyed such advantages and began to hit her mercilessly. They said: "Intruder; you have stolen Ochún's affection away from us. We will kill you. Ochún will have no choice but to love us. Take that and that." And they beat her violently.

"Ouch, ouch," cried the defenseless pumpkin. The pumpkin

managed to escape. She ran away and swiftly reached Ochún's house. She hammered desperately on the door.

"What is that banging?" asked Orúmbila, Ochún's husband.

"Let's see who it is," said his wife, and she went to open the door.

The pumpkin said, "Let me take refuge in your house, for they want to kill me."

"Oh, you have escaped from the garden? Come in."

The pumpkin told her mistress of the others' envy and jealously. She begged her to allow her to live in her house as she feared the violence of the others would kill her. It was not fair since she was the finest of them all. The most natural thing should be that she would live so as to excel and be able to enjoy the good things of life.

Ochún said, "Sleep peacefully; they won't bother you anymore."

The pumpkin settled down in the bed between the husband and wife. But halfway through the night Orúmbila woke up and said to the pumpkin, "Sleep on the floor, because I'm not comfortable."

The pumpkin said nothing and settled down under the bed. In the morning she got up and said to Ochún, "Your husband doesn't like me."

"Don't worry; I will help you with everything," said her mistress. And then she headed for her bedroom, took a sharp, shiny sickle, and set out for the pumpkin garden. She cut away all the reeds, stabbing at them violently while saying: "Take that for mistreating my favorite. Take that for incurring my anger."

When Ochún finished, she returned home. And the pumpkin said to her, "Thank you for honoring me in this way. Now I will be the only one who deserves your attention."

"From now on I will be your protector," said Ochún.

And the pumpkin said, "I will pay you back with interest."

At that time, Orúmbila was earning a lot of money throwing the Ifá.[21] When he finished his work, he put the coins in a sack and placed it in a secret hiding place. Then he went out. The pumpkin watched him do this and began to covet Orumbila's money. Thus, each afternoon when the old man had gone out, she went to the hiding place and stole a handful of coins, which she concealed in her bosom. The pumpkin grew extremely fat.

One day, Ochún, wishing to caress her, clasped her passionately to her chest. "Pumpkin, how fat you are!"

And the pumpkin made a jingling noise.

"What's that noise?" asked Ochún.

The pumpkin replied, "I'm robbing Orúmbila for you."

"You are clever, pumpkin. From now on you will be my moneybox." And the pumpkin was pleased to have her mistress as an accomplice.

Another day Echú turned up at the house and said, "I'm going to move in here until I see this couple ruined."

When the pumpkin heard this, she retorted, "Don't think that things will go so well for you."

"Who are you?" asked Echú.

"Me? Ochún's moneybox."

Echú began to hit her, and the pumpkin said, "I will give you a bottle of liquor if you stop hitting me."

"Done deal," said Echú.

The pumpkin brought him a bottle and said, "I will give you all the liquor you want if you don't get in Orúmbila's way. Treat the old man mercilessly."

"Very well."

From then on, Echú sprinkled the four corners of Orúmbila's house with a concoction of his invention, and the old man's business began to decline. Alarmed, Orúmbila consulted Ifá, but when he threw the chain it fell forming intricate patterns that the wise diviner could not decipher. Orúmbila resigned himself to bad luck. The day came when he did not even earn enough to eat.

The pumpkin said to Ochún, "Now the old man doesn't even earn enough to be able to steal a coin from him."

"The poor man! Bad luck, he's having a spell of bad luck. Shall we help him?"

"Don't count on me."

"Miser!" said Ochún angrily.

Echú and the pumpkin were discussing Orúmbila's fate. The pumpkin asked, "How far are you going to take the poor old man?"

"As far as I please."

"You should leave; you've already done him enough harm."

"Don't poke your nose into other people's affairs!"

"Hee, hee, hee," laughed the pumpkin, sure that Echú would not leave Orúmbila alone until he had destroyed him.

And she gave him more liquor. She was lavish with her generosity. One time Echú drank too much and fell down in the middle of the road. He did not realize that Ochún was approaching. Seeing him lying on the ground, Ochún prodded him gently with her foot, saying: "What are you doing here?"

Elegúa did not answer, and she prodded him more forcefully. "What are you doing here?"

Elegúa slowly opened his eyes and answered: "Ask the pumpkin."

The pumpkin, when questioned, said: "I had no idea he was

around, I haven't seen him hereabouts."

Ochún said: "You have been plotting with Echú." She slapped her twice and left.

When Orúmbila returned at nightfall with a wild expression on his face and sunken cheeks, like a ghost, he fell into a seat and said: "I'm dying!"

Ochún asked him: "Haven't you eaten?"

Orúmbila did not answer. Ochún thought that Icú had taken him away. Desperately she picked up a weapon and went to take her revenge on the pumpkin. The pumpkin ran and shouted: "You have fattened me up with Orúmbila's money and now you want to kill me!"

Ochún finally caught her and with a single stab of the knife, cut her in two. All the gold spilled out at Orúmbila's feet.

The old man, seeing the gold, cried: "Yalorde, you were the mistress of the ogúo!"[22]

Orúmbila's Parrots

Old Orúmbila, the Ifá diviner, was respected for his prestige and wisdom. As the result of a special favor from Olofi, he married Ochún, a woman of warrior stock. She was a beautiful girl who men found irresistibly attractive. She tempted them using subtle power of oñí,[23] the charm she used to captivate Olofi himself.

For the convenience of his profession, Orúmbila installed his wife in a mansion situated on a vast plain. It was easily accessible to the aleyos who came to discuss their misfortunes and to receive the embó[24] that would improve their luck. The aleyos came from afar in a long caravan that traversed the most arduous routes. Orúmbila's prestige was such that everyone made sacrifices in order to hear him speak comforting words and to live in accordance with that which destiny had ordained.

Orúmbila made plenty of money. He had enough to keep the greedy Ochún in sumptuous style. By nature she was fickle and given to deceit. They lived happily. They had a nice home, a good income, and enjoyable pastimes, but one thing worried Orúmbila. Every day his sex drive was decreasing, and Ochún, who was young and proud of her sexuality, demanded from him what he could not give her. "Let's go to bed," Ochún would demand. And he obliged her with his flagging virility. "What a man Olofi has given me," his wife complained, and her eyes filled with tears. Orúmbila understood that Ochún was a young woman. One day she would look to a younger man to provide her with what he could only offer her in a hazy memory of his younger days. He expected that the time would come when his spouse would spend in the arms of another the reserves of pleasure that he had caused her to accumulate.

That day came. Deep in the forest, his domain from one end to the other, lived the warrior Ogún Arere, the uncouth king of metalworkers. He intimidated his neighbors simply by tramping heavily through the land over which he reigned. Ogún Arere would only enjoy a woman once. He would use them violently and then push them away cruelly. But Ogún did not dare to be so impetuous with Ochún, as one day she had given him delicious pleasure.

Ogún said to her: "Woman, visit me always, I will give you expensive presents."

Ochún's various love affairs made her forget the incident, and they did not meet again. Her marital disaster with Orúmbila refreshed Ochún's memory, and she thought about the warrior and his powerful exuberance and wild energy when enjoying a woman.

One morning, Ochún, elegantly attired with five scarves tied round her waist, seven necklaces jingling at her neck, and smeared all over with honey, took the road to the forest to look for the metalworking king. At the foot of a leafy ceiba tree she found him lying on the grass in a deep slumber. Ochún began to undress swiftly. Naked, her body smeared and gleaming as it reflected the sun's rays, she began to dance while she sang a song of desire:

O-lo oñí oooh
Yeyé oñí oh.
Oñí abeeeee!

Ogún suddenly woke up. When he saw her he exclaimed: "Yalordé!" He tried to embrace her, but Ochún slipped nimbly away and danced dizzily until she fells exhausted into Ogún's arms.

"Ochún, you haven't changed."

"We will see each other every day."

Filled with foreboding, Orúmbila divined for himself. The chain gave him some indication of the betrayal. Orúmbila waited cautiously.

One afternoon when Ochún returned, she heard birds fluttering inside her house. She advanced swiftly and silently and saw that the house was full of parrots. Holding her breath, she listened to the cacophonous chatter of the parrots. The parrots were saying: "When will the adulteress return?"

"She'll be here sometime. We will tell him everything."

Ochún did not act foolishly. She went into the living room, pretending to be very happy. "Oh, how kind Orúmbila is. He's filled my house with parrots," she said.

The parrots watched her. "My parrots, would you like to eat?"

"Yes."

"Yes."

Ochún gave them otí[25] mixed with oñí and said to them softly: "Omoyú lepe-lepe."[26]

On that occasion not much happened. When Orúmbila arrived, the parrots said: "Ochún did not go out. Ochún is more virtuous than you think."

Orúmbila was not reassured by the parrots' declaration. He was aware of his wife's cunning. Orúmbila waited.

Ochún said to him: "How happy I am with my parrots! They amuse me in your absence."

"That is why I brought them."

But Orúmbila waited.

One day the master of the house arrived home and noticed that the parrots were immobile, in a deep sleep. He made a lot of noise to wake them up, but to no avail. The parrots kept on sleeping. Nothing could waken them. In a moment of absent-mindedness Ochún had added too much otí, more than she should, to the bird-seed. The man said nothing; he remained silent.

His wife said: "What's wrong with my little parrots; why are they so fast asleep?"

"Because they've had too much to eat."

Orúmbila did not say anything more. At night they went to bed. Orúmbila could not do anything, nor could Ochún. They were worried.

The following morning, Orúmbila said: "Wife, go to the forest and bring me oguedé. I have a craving for them."

Ochún went without saying anything. As soon as her husband was sure that he wouldn't be surprised by his wife, he went over to the parrots and daubed their beaks with epó,[27] saying: "Now you will have no choice but to tell the truth."

Orúmbila devoted himself to his work. He divined for the aleyos with his usual impassiveness. When Ochún came back, the old man took the bananas and began to peel them calmly. As he ate he said: "Don't give the parrots anything to eat. I have already done so. You'd better see to the housework."

"Very well."

When Orúmbila went off, Ochún very discreetly gave the parrots the birdseed mixed with oñí or otí, muttering the words: "Omoyú lepe-lepe." And she went to meet the warrior Ogún-Arere, whom she told of Orúmbila's suspicions. The metalworking king responded by piling gold into her hands. Ochún set off for her large house, expecting that everything would be resolved to her advantage because she had a lot of faith in the power of her oñí.

Orúmbila was calmly waiting for her. As soon as she entered the house, the parrots begin to chatter with a deafening racket. They were saying:

"The adulteress has arrived."

"She has come from seeing Ogún Arere."

"Orúmbila, your wife is cheating on you!"

"Kill her!"

Ochún began to hit them furiously, crying: "Traitors, toadies!"

Parrots always tell the truth.

 # The Sacrifice

They say that when Ochún was in her prime she used to enjoy herself at güemilere whenever she chose, boldly confronting the gaze of the lads who looked admiringly at her swaying body. Her waist was narrower than that of a woman of more noble birth. Her fingers tapered like the blade of a sharp dagger. But even with expert wooing, no man managed to have the pleasure of lightly brushing against the skirt of that omordé, more cunning than sensible. Sometimes on hot nights Ochún would allow herself to be pursued by handsome, well-built lads whom she brought into her ilé and granted brief nights of pleasure.

The omordé's waist was so slim that it could be encircled by a child's tiny arms. Her hips were so narrow that, when her arms were folded, she could pass through a slender hoop from head to toe.

One day she turned up at the güemilere presided over by Changó, the handsome drummer, whose fame was recounted in tales that passed from village to village. Ochún asked permission to speak a few admiring words to the most dexterous of the drummers. She went over to the drums and, bowing her head, ceremoniously said to him: "Emí,[28] you are the greatest of the drummers.

Please deign to visit me."

Changó interrogated her: "Who should I ask for?"

"You should ask for Yalorde, your humble servant."

"Oh, Yalorde?" said Changó, and he thought for a few seconds. Suddenly he replied: "You are not worthy of my attention," and he continued to play his drums.

From that moment on, Ochún, wearing the most outrageous clothes, did not miss a single day of the güemilere that was presided over by the indolent youth who dared to humiliate her in front of all her admirers. On one occasion she took off her tunic and danced right beside the drums. Her whole body was smeared with oñí that dripped from her narrow fingers and fell to the ground like drops of gold. Everyone watched fascinated as the nimblest dancer at the güemilere moved restlessly.

Changó calmly dripped some oñí onto his face and said gravely: "Cofiadeno, omordé."[29]

Ochún ran away with her head bowed and two tears filling her deep black eyes.

The following day Ochún went back to Changó. "Please deign to share the bed of the most desired woman ever born," she said.

"Ochún, leave me alone," he answered and went on presiding over the celebrations.

Despite this, Ochún persevered. On one occasion, choosing the moment when the drummer was resting from the exhaustion of the night, she slid silently onto his mat and, using delicate flattery, prepared the youth who could not resist her extremely skillful caresses.

When they finished, Changó said: "Omordé, you're not good at handling men." And he turned his back on her.

This partial victory of Ochún broke the ice, and they continued to see each other on the nights that favor lovemaking under the full moon, which revealed the accessible paths of the forest, or they coupled on the damp grass of the open spaces, because, in spite of everything, Changó did not give Ochún an inch.

He humiliated her frequently: "Ochún, you are not worthy of my bed; you don't know how to make love to men."

"You are clumsy and as sluggish as an elephant. You stay stuck to me like a slug at the moment when any prudent woman moves away."

Ochún bore this stoically like someone betting on a hunch. But the moment arrived when fortune turned its back on Changó, and he became less popular at the güemilere. He regarded his downfall impassively. His pride made him abandon his job rather than suffer the ridicule of passing unnoticed in the place of his greatest successes, and he settled in an ilé far from the raucous sound of the drums.

Ochún went there and comforted him. She gave up all her possessions and took with her just one dress that she fastidiously washed every day in a bend in the river. Ochún took her tunic to the river so often that, once white, it became yellow and washed out. From then on, Changó began to feel love for Yalorde.

Ogún Arere's Trap

Old babalochas[30] tell of how Ogún Arere, who ruled over the immense forest, selfishly wanted to keep for himself all the profits from the bountiful harvests and incalculable riches the forest hid in its interior. Thus no one was allowed to traverse its paths. So as to avoid the bother of chasing after them, he concealed traps in the dry grass along the pathways. Many men of an adventurous nature had interred their foolhardiness in attempting to defy the will of the mighty farmer.

Each morning Ogún Arere inspected all his traps. Bare-chested and with a machete slung through his belt, he walked with heavy, swaggering steps, using a long stick to push aside the dry grass. When he saw the deep holes, his bloodthirsty nature was satisfied to see how many men lay there packed together, struggling against death with no hope of any reward and not having had a chance to take their leave of life bravely.

This practice continued for many years. It ensured that the farmer's territory remained undisturbed. He felt confident of his authority when he saw that the traps contained old and fossilized bones.

However, one day Olofi, whose authority could not be questioned, ordered Orúmbila, his most trusted servant, to go into the forest to collect some of Ogún Arere's obí.[31] Orúmbila trembled from head to toe. But he had no alternative but to obey. As he was skinny, he thought he would be able to slip safely past the hidden traps. The following morning he set off with a sack of provisions over his shoulder to trust his life to fate. He became hopelessly lost and began shouting in the forest. But his cries echoed feebly around its cavernous depths and could not be heard outside the forest. Old Orúmbila understood that his agony had begun. He lowered his head onto his chest and was resigned to die. The earth began to eat away his flesh, which was already wasted. Little by little only the sorry remains of a human were left; flies were buzzing around it, and worms lay in wait.

All that remained of Orúmbila was the spirit of a man when, one morning, three cheerful and talkative women were going through the field picking flowers along the pathways. They stepped unwittingly on Ogún Arere's graveyards. The traps, many now laid bare, were lined with loose bones. The women walked lightly over the grassy surface, revealing the long line of graves with their harvest of skulls and entwined bones.

One of the women was Obatalá, a gentle, serene girl; the second was Yemayá, plump and lissome; and the third was Ochún, nimble, frivolous, and alluring. She went in front. Either to show that she was unmoved by the grisly spectacle or because she knew of no other way to subdue her emotions than with a song, she began to sing softly, waving her hands in the air:

> Yeyeo oñí oh . . .
> oñí abell
> securé a la yumó! . . .

Oñí abé.
Securé a la idó! . . .
Oñí abé.
Securé ibucolé! . . .
Oñí abeee . . .

Meanwhile the others stifled cries of horror, and their bodies trembled when they saw the new traps. The three women were startled to hear a loud snore coming from one of the holes. It was Orúmbila's death rattle. At that moment the three women leaned over and saw him, tall, thin, and bent, with his nails clawing the earth as if he was grasping at his last hope.

"My abure,[32] it's Orúmbila!" Yemayá said to her sister Ochún.

"Let's save him!" said Obatalá.

Ochún, untying the five handkerchiefs she normally wore at her belt, made a strong cord and a lasso, and between the three of them they lifted out the old man, who was half dead.

They carried him before Olofi. He received him without much surprise and did not seem to be very interested in Orúmbila's mishap. He said to Ochún: "Go and deal with Ogún Arere."

To Yemayá he said: "Liven him up!" And she made him drink a bottle of liquor.

At Olofi's request, Obatalá also took him in her arms. Murmuring some words in his ear, she calmed and revived him, for she is the mistress of human understanding.

Halfway through the afternoon, Ochún entered the forest and ran from one end to the other shouting and attempting to attract the farmer's attention. When he heard her, Ogún Arere irritably pulled out his machete and went in pursuit of her. But when he found her he changed his mind and asked her in a perfectly normal voice:

"Omordé, what are you looking for?"

Ochún, who had greeted him lying naked on the ground, let him know her intentions with a salacious gesture, and she replied: "Nothing, I have come to enjoy myself with you." And they had sexual intercourse.

Taking out a bottle of liquor that she had concealed, the woman then said: "Drink this liquor."

Ogún Arere, stunned by the ruthlessness of what had just taken place, obediently tipped up the bottle and became completely drunk.

Ochún quickly ran to his hiding place, stole all his money, and ran away.

Ogún Arere, filled with shame, found he no longer needed to take precautions and allowed free access to his domain.

Deception

Olofi granted a simple obiní called Ogún Arere, who was sturdy and cantankerous, the honor of being the supreme lord of the immense tracts of the forest. Thus he was beyond reach of all social relations and only had contact with his fellow men when he wished to test his strength and impose his authority. He guarded with an uncommon zeal the area between his domain and the neighboring villages. No living creature could attempt to cross it without risking being cruelly affronted.

Although Ogún Arere was able to conquer women and give them maximum satisfaction, he also turned his unseemly temper on them. He embraced them powerfully and vigorously and then, after possessing them, would beat them violently. No woman could boast of having visited him more than once. Nevertheless, on dark nights the omordés slipped through the forest and lay in wait for him on the grass, where the farmer would take them brutally and savagely.

On account of the legends about the rather ungallant habits of this powerful farmer, on the night of a moon that seemed to throw torrents of light into the dark forest, Yemayá Saramaguá,[33] a lively and vigorous girl uninitiated in the mysteries of love, entered the wood. She went down paths with hazardous intersections breaking the silence all the while with a song that lamented the sadness of her body in the first flower of womanhood:

> Acolona oooh!
> Aeee!
> Dale yaluma oh!
> Dale ayaba mío,
> Oñí abeee!
> Si Yemayá ta secú secú.
> Si Yemayá ta cuelé cuelé
> Epooooo!
> Ucineba oooh!
> Aeeee!

Ogún Arere, armed with a machete of gigantic proportions, half naked and displaying a mop of rough, curly hair, was wandering about when the echo of her voice made him stop suddenly. He headed in the direction of the bold young woman's song.

Yemayá Saramaguá saw him coming. Her whole body trembled slightly, and she cried in a trembling voice: "Hey Aguanillí!"[34]

He settled down to wait for her in a turn of the path. The girl went along the track, and Ogún Arere threw himself on her. He raped her in jerky spasms until Yemayá, trembling all over, rubbed her exhausted body against the man's strong muscles. He pushed her away, but the girl was inflamed with desire. She came back and embraced him, murmuring: "Aguanillí, keep on filling me up. I'm not satisfied!"

Ogún Arere disengaged himself. Holding her by her delicate waist, he threw her to the ground. But the maiden, whose desire was not diminished by physical pain, stood up swiftly and went stubbornly toward the farmer. He took a step back and, brandishing his machete and chopping the air, threatened her angrily: "I will have to kill you, insatiable bitch!"

The girl gave up in the face of such opposition. Filled with terror, she started running to the edge of the forest and went to her ilé. Yemayá was desolate and had a heavy heart. She still carried the marks of Ogún Arere's powerful virility on her thighs. She ran to look for her experienced sister, Ochún. In between sobs she told of her misfortune and asked her to use her cunning to punish the farmer's brazen deed. "My abure," she said, "a man has humiliated me. After he possessed me, Ogún Arere left without satisfying my desire."

"Don't worry, I will bring him to you at night so that you may have your pleasure."

Armed with a plate brimming with oñí, Ochún went along the long path leading to the forest that was crossed by little streams. She went as far as the place where the mighty river flows, heaving warily like a gigantic boa. Ochún, who is called Yalorde in güemilere songs, passed through the dense jungle, clearing a path with her arms and filling the forest with her song:

> Securé a la yumó oh!
> Securé a la idó oh
> Yeyé oooh
> Oñí abeee!
> Securé a la yumó oh,
> Securé a la idó oh,
> Yeyé oñí oooh!

When they met, Ogún Arere, fiercely eager, tried to seize her arms, but the woman swiftly evaded him and placed her plate of honey on the ground to await his next move. The farmer, who was looking daggers at her, was overcome with rage, and he repeated the action. The girl slipped away easily and danced before him freely, defying his attempts to embrace her. The farmer clumsily clutched at air, attempting to grasp the güemilere dancer's beautiful body.

She stole away, swaying like a stalk of maize in the wind. In the frenzy of the dance, Ochún took one end of her skirt and spun quickly until it came off. She held it in her hands like a sail with the wind in it and let Ogún Arere see her curvaceous, sweaty, glistening body. The farmer stayed there, enraptured by that outrageous woman. Pausing in her dance, she took the plate of oñí and poured it over her body that now cried out for moments of love.

The farmer seized the moment and got on top of her, holding her by the waist. Ochún moved her hips restlessly like a trapped fish. Once more she mocked him, laughing loudly enough to fill the entire wood. Ogún Arere, panting, his hands smeared with the charm, was clumsy and bewildered. The omordé, seeing she had won, cunningly entered the deep forest. She went ahead, singing her song:

> Yeyé oñi oh.
> Oñí abee!

Aguanillí followed her as meekly as a lamb. When they reached the edge of the forest, she lay down and artfully revealed her ample bosom and aroused body.

Ogún Arere took her noisily and as greedily as a miser.

"Omordé, you have not left me entirely satisfied," he said, half exhausted.

Ochún replied: "Let's do it indoors," and she dragged him to Yemayá Saramaguá's ilé, where she was lying on her mat, waiting patiently.

It was a dark night, and the farmer didn't notice the other woman. He settled down with Ochún in the bed. She got up from his arms and left him with her sister, who silently replaced her all night long. "Will you come back, obiní?" Yemayá asked the next morning.

Realizing he had been tricked, Ogún Arere hit her furiously and went away.

Here ends the story in which Ochún, the most beautiful girl at the güemilere, violated the strict principles of the formidable Ogún Arere.

Cunning

Ogún Arere, the lord of iron and a warrior by profession, appeared before his sworn enemy, Changó de Ima. He suggested calling a truce in one of the long drawn-out battles that they frequently fought, sometimes for completely trivial reasons, sometimes to win the honors Olofi bestowed on the victor. But these proud and majestic warriors mainly fought to indulge their warlike natures.

On this occasion Ogún Arere said: "Changó, I am tired of fighting; let's rest until the next moon."

"Very well, I accept," replied Changó, using his sharp, shining machete to cut the slender stem of a bush with an affected abandon.

Ogún Arere, making an effort to be polite, bowed his heroic head and said insincerely: "Your good sense greatly pleases me. Had it not been so, your death would soon have been a tangible fact."

"I see that you are a braggart," replied Changó calmly, cutting a hair with his shining machete.

"Well, Changó, I have not come looking for a fight. Instead we should take advantage of this truce by passing the time somehow."

"What game do you suggest?"

"Well, let's go to the beach and we'll see who's best at collecting shells."

"Oh, I'll beat you! I'm a hundred times quicker than you."

"Then let's bet something on it. The winner will take the loser's fortune. Do you accept?"

"With the greatest of pleasure."

"Then we'll meet tomorrow on the shore."

Ogún Arere left him and set off for the house of Oyá, the keeper of the cemetery. He proposed the following: "I want you to rent me Icú early tomorrow morning."

"That depends on whether you pay me a decent amount."

Ogún Arere handed her six bags of gold, and the deal was closed. The following morning Icú would simply turn up on the beach.

The wager began, and the rivals industriously gathered the shells that were scattered on the sand. From time to time they watched each other suspiciously out of the corner of their eyes. They put the shells in the bags that hung from their arms, moving in opposite directions, bent over, engrossed in their not altogether honorable task.

Changó gathered the shells unhurriedly, every so often humming softly and tauntingly:

> Ogún Arere,
> Meyi meyi mellizo
> Ogún Arereeee.

And just when he was at his most tuneful, Icú came and kicked him on the backside. Changó turned angrily and bumps into Death,

who was serene and enigmatic.

"Hee, hee, hee," laughed Death.

Changó dropped his sack, performed three cartwheels, and ran off faster than a buck to hide.

That night he got a visit from Ogún Arere, who provocatively threw two sacks full of shells at his feet. Changó, the loser, bowed his head in shame and handed over all his wealth.

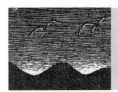

Ochosi de Mata

Olofi, the father of heaven and earth, called his assistant, Orúmbila, and spoke to him thus: "Orúmbila, it would please me if you fetch me a quail."

"A quail?" replied Orúmbila, astonished. "No human being has ever managed to trap one."

"I command you to find me a quail."

"It is difficult, Olofi; set me another task."

"Fetch me the quail from within the world's boundaries."

"Very well, you shall have it," replied Orúmbila, realizing that any attempt to dissuade his master would be futile.

The next morning, Orúmbila went into the forest with his quiver full of arrows and his gleaming bow. He began walking along a long path that went deep into the dense forest. Then he crossed mountains that were arduous to climb. A thousand times he confronted the quail, a thousand times he shot his bow in vain, and as many times saw his attempt fail. He went along every path and used up all his arrows, and the quail mocked his skill as a hunter.

Orúmbila became discouraged. When the sun began to go down and night was falling, dark and full of a thousand omens, Orúmbila, tired and downcast, took the path that led to the villages.

In the villages the people noticed the traveler with his empty quiver. He was covered in mud, more discouraged than exhausted by his prolonged effort, and had a detached expression. Orúmbila looked at everyone worriedly, trying to find in each the person who would be able to get him out of his predicament. From time to time he stopped in front of groups of people and said: "Olofi wants a quail. Whoever gets him one will receive powerful aché."

Some of them, noticing his defeated look, laughed in his face and went away. Others replied: "You are asking a lot. We can't fulfil your ambitions."

Orúmbila began to despair more and more. He went from village to village, and his footsteps raised clouds of dust, as if Orúmbila wished to punish the earth. He reached places where brave men were able to perform the boldest feats, and he came into contact with real hunters who had made an art out of their trade. The only answer he got was:

"We can't."

"We can't."

Orúmbila no longer had any idea of time. Night gave way to day and day to night. Once, twice, three times. And the traveler, covered in mud, unhappy and frustrated, heard only these discouraging words from people's lips:

"Your endeavor is ridiculous."

"Why don't you earn the aché for yourself?"

Deciding to go back and await from Olofi the punishment he deserved for his failure, Orúmbila took a long, narrow path where the echo of the forest's sounds faded. He walked slowly and wearily. He went deep into the wood and heard the sound of distant drumming that resonated through his entire body. He headed quickly toward the place it was coming from. As he got closer, his body vibrated and his feet pulled him along as he were gliding effortlessly to the beat of that music. His spirits lifted. Orúmbila became a new man. Close by, he heard the song very clearly:

> Ochosi aqui-l-odara
> A la mata dé.
> Ochosi de Mata,
> Oqué oqué
> Yambere iloraaaaaa
> Y de mataaaaa!
> Oqué oqué!

He reached the place where the drums were reverberating. It was the güemilere with drums decked with red ribbons to greet Changó, blue ones to pay tribute to Yemayá, yellow to greet Ochún, and white for Obatalá. The great party of the saints. Everyone wore festive white sackcloth and beaded necklaces that glinted in the sunlight. Bit by bit, the drums lifted the spirits of those present. They got faster and faster, playing a thousand notes. Everyone fell to the ground gyrating voluptuously and then rose up beating the air with their hips and singing:

> Yambere iloraaaaa
> A la mata deeee.

Orúmbila approached the drums. He surrendered to the insistent music, and, twitching his body like a snake, he gave himself up to the party.

The most striking people there were a woman, a real woman who swayed and danced tirelessly and as delicately as a palm tree, waving her arms majestically in the air. It was Ochún, queen of the güemilere. And also a stout, manly lad who danced with the girl, feigning an amorous devotion that was dispersed with the sounding of each note. This was Ochosi de Mata.

When the party had quieted down a little, Orúmbila asked: "What is the reason for such merriment?"

"We are honoring Ochosi de Mata, the greatest hunter," they replied.

Then Orúmbila said: "I am Orúmbila, Olofi's assistant. I would like to speak to him."

Those present bowed down until their foreheads touched the ground, making moforibale,[35] and they hastened to call Ochosi.

He appeared.

"Ochosi," said Orúmbila, "Olofi has deigned to appoint you the hunter of the quail."

"An honor that I deserve, you shall have it tomorrow."

"Good."

The güemilere went on until the sun showed its glowing face. In the late morning, Ochosi went to the countryside and caught the quail. He went back to his house and left it in the care of his mother. And he informed Orúmbila, who asked him: "Have you performed your errand?"

"Of course."

They both headed for Ochosi's house. When they arrived, he made Orúmbila wait in the doorway while he went inside. A few moments later he came back with a distraught expression and trembling with rage: "They have stolen it!" he exclaimed, starting to walk to and fro, shouting: "My iyare, you know what happened to the quail!"

"I don't know, nor do I care," she replied.

"You have deceived me," Orúmbila said calmly.

"No," cried Ochosi, desperately.

"Ochosi," Orúmbila said in the same tone, "I will give you another chance. If you bring it to me you will receive aché from Olofi; if not, you will pay dearly."

"I will bring it to you, Orúmbila!"

"Good, I will be waiting."

They parted company.

Ochosi, raging and taking powerful strides, broke through the forest in search of the quail. Eventually he found it and caught it once more. "This time you will definitely not trick me," he said, and put it in his bag.

At once he looked for Orúmbila. "I have it now; let's take it to Olofi," he said.

They followed a mountainous path and, heading toward the top of the hill where Olofi's white dwelling lay, climbed until they disappeared from view. They arrived and stopped in the doorway. Orúmbila knocked three times and waited. Olofi appeared with majesty and pomp, and they both prostrated themselves on the floor.

"Here is the quail, father," said Orúmbila humbly.

Olofi took it in his hands and stroked it gently while watching Ochosi de Mata out of the corner of his eye. Suddenly he adopted a serious pose and, stretching out his right arm, said: "Ochosi de Mata, I name you king of the hunters!"

"Thank you; you have given me a rank that I deserve," said Ochosi, prostrating himself. Then he got up nimbly and, taking his bow, fired an arrow at random. And he said: "Olofi, may the arrow stick in the heart of the person who stole the quail."

"So be it," they answered.

Ochosi de Mata went down to earth. When he entered his home he gave a cry of horror and ran out, hands on his head, saying: "Olofi, you have killed my mother. My iyare! It was you!"

His mother was stretched out with the arrow in her chest.

Ochosi de Mata stopped in front of a tree and let himself fall down heavily. He was deeply distressed. He lowered his head and threw the quiver of arrows to the ground. He gave himself up to weeping. He shed floods of tears. As he was a man of determination, he resolved not to use the power Olofi had granted him if it would discredit it.

One day when Olofi had ordered him not to go into the forest to hunt, Ochosi went into the woods. He began to shoot arrows to the right and to the left. Suddenly he saw a fine specimen approaching and took better aim. But as he fired, the animal turned into Odú-dua. The hunter was so afraid that he remained there petrified, holding out his bow in the action of shooting. Thus Ochosi de Mata became a legend.

Here it ends.

Orúmbila's Moquenquen

There was a time when there was no more delicious morsel for Olofi than the steaming, grilled flesh of a lad or a nubile and well-bred maiden, carefully selected from the most distinguished families. On one occasion, his faithful servant Orúmbila was on his way to the village where they were waiting to hand over the specimen intended for his master's lunch when he met a fine-looking boy wandering round the outskirts. To save himself a long walk, he caught him and presented him to Olofi on a shining dish. When Olofi tasted the first mouthful, he liked its fine taste and he asked: "Orúmbila, what kind of meat is this?"

"It's moquenquen meat," he said.

"Well, it's delicious. From now on give it to me instead of the other."

Pleased with the happy outcome of his laziness, the old man went down to the villages. Gathering everyone together, he explained Olofi's changed tastes. He exaggeratedly praised his refined palate and urged everyone present to bear in mind the gift of the moquenquen, which he would deliver to his destination.

Those assembled said in unison: "Of course; we will be honored to procreate in order to sustain Olofi."

Thus, in the days that followed, Orúmbila had only to say: "I have come for Olofi's food," and they would hand over the boy, saying: "Take the family's finest offspring."

But this new departure so whetted Olofi's appetite that when he finished one he would say: "Orúmbila, this morsel hasn't filled me up; bring me another."

The old man obliged him by bringing him another boy. And he must have eaten up to five at one sitting. This annoyed the villagers, whose wives found themselves in the humiliating predicament of bearing children simply to feed the appetite of the unscrupulous Olofi. And they gathered together to discuss how to prevent their children meeting such a terrible fate.

The omordés said: "We should not have to give birth in order that lazybones may eat"

And the obiní said: "We should hide them in the forest." And that is what happened.

On the following day, Orúmbila arrived at a door, and they forestalled him. saying: "If you have come for the moquenquen then you will have to go away empty-handed."

"But I have come for another reason."

Then the omordé started to cry and said: "Orúmbila, the moquenquen was taken by Icú last night."

Orúmbila left. The next day he went to another ilé and got the same answer: "Death has taken the moquenquen away."

And thus, on the days that followed, the old man was greeted with the same answer while Olofi fasted. Until, on the fourth day, no longer able to contain his hunger, he summoned his assistant and said to him angrily: "My guts are sticking to my backbone. You must bring me food right away!"

Realizing that he could not answer back, Orúmbila went out

and, after walking to and fro in search of a solution, he headed for Eleguá's ilé. "I need you to get me a moquenquen," he said.

"You will have to pay me dearly."

"I will give you a bottle of liquor."

"Done deal," answered Eleguá. And he went into the forest and surprised the crowd of children who were playing happily in the bushes, having completely forgotten their former destiny. They had gotten fatter and become stronger and more lively in that peaceful, safe place.

Eleguá, pretending to be good, mixed with them, but the moquenqueré greeted him warily: "What are you doing here, old dodderer?"

"Nothing; I have come to teach you an amusing game."

The boys, seeing him so good-natured and vague, begin to trust him, and they said innocently: "Well, let's see this game."

"Let's make a bet on who is the best runner in the savannah," answered Eleguá. "I will race against one of you."

"Come on, decrepit old man, you can't even crawl," answered the boys, laughing in his face.

Eleguá, without turning a hair, insisted, and one of them finally agreed to test his stamina against him. At the signal they started to run. Halfway the old man pretended to be lame; he fell down, and his opponent overtook him.

The other boys went up to him and said teasingly: "See how you've worn yourself out?" And they started laughing at him again.

Eleguá stood up with difficulty and he asked them to give him another chance, claiming that he tripped over an unseen obstacle. His opponent agreed. But this time he ran swiftly, leaving the moquenquen behind.

The others who were anxiously watching the spectacle were

amazed. The old man surprised them by running as swiftly as a gazelle, and the boy, out of breath, lost speed, little by little. Then they complained: "You have won unfairly. The moquenquen was tired," they all cried.

The old man replied: "Very well, all of you race against me then."

"We'll do that," said the protesters. And, lining up alongside him, they started running.

Eleguá cunningly sometimes let them get in front and sometimes ran alongside them, spurring them on as he gradually gained their confidence and led them imperceptibly down a path that ended in an enclosure. At this point he ran faster than they. The moquenqueré, eager to beat him, ran blindly until their little bodies crashed into the barriers and they fell down in a confused heap. Then the old man hurried to block the entrance, saying: "Now I will hand you all over to Orúmbila." And he ran to find him.

When Orúmbila saw the moquenqueré squirming in fear and confusion, he handed the liquor to Eleguá and said: "I see that you are crafty. I will give you all the liquor you want."

"We'll discuss that another time, for now, take what is your due."

In the enclosure, the boys wept and moaned, letting out piercing cries that sometimes turned into a single deafening and pitiful shriek. Only one boy remained calm and instead of complaining, walking to and fro quietly, as if all this were quite normal. Suddenly he began to sing softly and melodiously:

> Orúmbila talardé
> Babá moforibale
> Orúmbila talardé
> Babá moforibaleee

The person referred to in the song was startled. Quickly opening the fence, he took the boy in his arms and asked him: "Who taught you to sing like that?"

"My iyare."

"What is her name?" Orúmbila asked.

The boy replied: "I don't know who my father is, nor my mother. I was born with the song and I sing it because it is nice."

Orúmbila said nothing. He took him before Olofi and urged him to cease his cannibalistic yearnings, saying: "This moquenquen is my son whom Ochún abandoned. I looked for him everywhere without finding him. Now by chance your excesses have placed him in my hands. This is why I want all the moquenqueré to be free from being devoured by your cravings."

Olofi answered him coldly: "Since you have obliged me to fast, I will eat this boy. From now on, I will seek other forms of sustenance. Your wish is granted."

And Orúmbila served him his son on a colorful dish.

Orúmbila and Icú

A very thin and unhealthy-looking omordé, visibly disturbed by some great affliction, arrived one day at Orúmbila's door. Her face was soaked in tears, and she was sighing deeply. Falling to her knees, unable to contain her weeping, she spoke these faltering words: "Orúmbila, Icú is prowling around my house. Don't let him take my good, tender boy away."

Seeing her so downcast, Orúmbila said: "Go into the forest and gather four baskets of okra. I will wait for you at your house."

The old man immediately set out for the ilé. He goes into the bedroom and leans over the bed where the boy, making every effort to fight off death, was lying. With a small piece of chalk he marked a cross on his forehead that burned with fever. Then he waited for the woman to come back. Spreading the okra on the ground, he covered it over until it looked like a green carpet. He ordered the omordé to leave and, positioning himself in a corner, awaited Icú's arrival.

Death entered in a martial fashion. But no sooner had she taken a few steps than she lost her balance and began to totter, slipping on the green floor. Her footsteps exploded the okra pods with a dry crackling sound. Finding herself in a position quite unseemly for someone of her rank, she made feeble efforts to grasp invisible supports in the darkness until, thrown completely off her center of gravity, she fell to the ground noisily, like a sack of pebbles. She let out a cry of indignation: "Wheee!"

Orúmbila immediately came out of his hiding place and, cracking a poplar switch, hit her vigorously. Faced with this punishment, Icú managed to stand up, hopping to and fro and swelling to enormous proportions. But the old man continued hitting her with his whip until he reduced her to a tiny dot.

Icú had no choice but to look for a way out. Jumping up, she climbed into an empty bottle that was lying in a corner of the house. Orúmbila put a cork on the hiding place and chastised her more vigorously, saying: "Icú, now you are in my power!"

She replied: "Release me from this humiliation, and I will readily accept your terms."

The old man took her to the moquenquen, whose closed eyelids avoided the prisoner's deadly gaze. Showing her the cross, he said: "Do you see that sign? Well, that means that whoever has it is under my care, and therefore you must respect him. Do you agree to my terms?"

"I will gladly accept them," said Icú.

And Orúmbila let her go.

The moquenquen was completely cured. Since then, the superstition remains that on her jaunts, Death tends to lodge in bottles. That is why it is dangerous to leave them unstopped.

Here I have said it all.

Obatalá and Orula

For a long time Obatalá had been noticing how imaginative Orula was. On more than one occasion he had considered handing over the command of the world to him. But, when he thought his plan over carefully, he decided against it. For, despite his good sense and the seriousness of all his deeds, Orula was too young for such an important mission.

One day, Obatalá wanted to discover whether Orula was as capable as he appeared. He ordered him to prepare the best meal that could be made. Orula listened to Obatalá's wishes. Without saying anything, he headed for the nearby market to buy a bull's tongue. He seasoned it and cooked it in such an unusual way that Obatalá, satisfied, licked his lips with pleasure. When the meal was over, Obatalá asked him why the tongue was the best meal that could be prepared.

Orula answered Obatalá: "With the tongue aché is granted. With it one praises things, one proclaims virtue, one exalts deeds and manners, and one also extols men."

When some time had gone by, Obatalá wanted Orula to prepare a meal for him again, but this time it should be the worst that could be made.

Orula went back to the market, bought a bull's tongue, cooked it, and presented it to Obatalá. When Obatalá saw it was the same meal that Orula had considered the best, he said to him: "Orula! How can it be that when you served me this meal you acknowledged that it was the best, and now you're presenting it as the worst?"

Orula answered: "Then I told you it was the best, but now I am telling you it is the worst, because with it one sells out and ruins people, one slanders them, one ruins their good name, and one commits the vilest deeds."

Obatalá was amazed by Orula's intelligence and precocity, and from that moment he handed over the command of the world to him.

The Legend of Icú

People speak of a time when no one died. As no creature living on earth died, the world became so overpopulated that it was impossible to take a step. The old people, wrinkled and shrunken, could neither walk nor die. They laboriously dragged their long white hair around. However, they solved the problem of their weakness by coming together like the industrious ants that move dry leaves in the woods. Up to twenty old people would join together to move a dry twig to keep the bonfire going. Forty were not enough to move a clay pot. Eighty would arrange to meet to cut a pumpkin, because they were very weak, not strong enough to do anything.

The young people invoked the gods and asked them to free them from the old people's uselessness. They were so insistent that Icú eventually listened their pleas. A deep voice, like the roaring of a hurricane, was heard in the distance, in the deepest and most remote part of the jungle. The young people came to meet the obliging Icú, who would solve the problem.

"It will rain for three days and three nights without stopping," said Icú from the depths of the forest, "and the waters will rise. The young and children must climb to the top floor of the houses as the rain will flood the fields. The earth will be a river that has no banks."

The young people answered Icú, very distressed, "Our houses don't have upper stories."

Icú spoke again: "Climb up onto the roof of your houses."

"The roof of our houses is made of palm leaves. It won't take the weight."

"Then," said Icú angrily, "climb into the treetops."

Icú's irate words were followed by thunder and the first rains. For three days and three nights it rained constantly. The clouds were like a broken pitcher. On the first day, the rain covered the roots and paths. On the second, the houses were hidden under water. On the dawn of the third day, the rainwater reached as high as the elephants' trunks and the giraffes.

The waters continued to rise slowly until they were as high as tigers must leap to catch monkeys. The earth was a sea without swell or coastline, with floating islands of broken branches. In the tops of the highest, leafiest trees the young people and children waited for the promise to be fulfilled.

On the morning of the first day, the old people, shivering with cold, tried to reach the high branches but were not able to because the overflowing water climbed the thick trunks of the baobabs and yagrumas more quickly than the slow movements of the numb old people.

When it cleared, on the dawn of the fourth day, in the light of a cloudless sky washed by the gods, the young people saw that there were no sickly, old people left in the world. Even the young also began to die, possibly because some did not manage climb up to the treetops in time.

Part Three

The Invisible Dog

At the beginning of the year 1770, Doña Ramonita Oramas, the widow of Solís, lived alone, poor and respectable in a little house some way from the Plaza de Armas in Matanzas. But Ramonita had a faithful companion in her solitude, an enormous white dog that she called Captain.

Ramonita sewed exquisitely and made sweetmeats and favors. She was received in all the best houses of the town for she was distantly related to the most distinguished families.

Every day of the year, in the pouring rain or oppressive heat, any curious neighbor could see Ramonita on her way to church accompanied by Captain. She went inside, and the dog lay in the doorway of the church waiting for his mistress. Daily mass and frequent communion were the stay and comfort of the brave heart of the industrious fifty-year-old widow.

Ramonita had a strange secret. She had asked the Holy Virgin to give her dog a long life so that Captain, her only companion, could be with her until she was summoned by death. Thus Ramonita was very moved one morning when she saw from her pew that Captain, breaking with his custom of waiting for her in the doorway, had entered the church. He stopped in front of a side altar where there was a statue of the Holy Virgin. After looking at the statue for a long while, he lay down in front of it. In the almost deserted church, no one saw Captain lying at the feet of the Virgin Mary. This unusual episode in Captain's life was witnessed only by his mistress, who interpreted it as an answer from the Holy Virgin to her plea for a long life for Captain.

No one was able to explain how it came about: Captain, Doña Ramonita's huge white dog, lay dead in the street in front of the church with his head split open.

Ramonita wept for Captain and prayed for him each day before the altar of the Virgin Mary. Three weeks after Captain's death, Ramonita heard a dog barking in the patio of her little house, the unmistakable bark of her deceased Captain. The insistent barking made Ramonita go out onto the patio. She saw Captain—yes, it was Captain, but transformed. His hair was a bright white like moonlight, and his eyes had become blue and luminous. Unafraid, Ramonita called the dog, and it came to her, wagging its tail joyfully, and licked her hands. Then it made itself invisible and disappeared.

January 1771 came, and on her deathbed Ramonita revealed that she saw Captain every day, transformed into a protector, able to be with her but invisible. And Ramonita maintained that she knew that the Virgin had granted eternal life to her dog, that she had made Captain an invisible friend to help the good people of Matanzas.

Ramonita, died and Ramonita's friends thought that the story she had told shortly before she died was just the delirium of a sick person who is about to die.

One night in March 1771, the teacher Don Pablo García (who had been brought from Havana by Alderman Waldo García de

Oramas, a distant relative of Ramonita) saw a huge dog with fleece as bright as moonlight and luminous blue eyes but that, as he watched, became invisible. The teacher, Don Pablo, talked a great deal about the dog that could make itself invisible. And the Alderman, hearing the teacher, began to think that the dog was Captain, and he remembered what they said Doña Ramonita Oramas had told them on the day she died.

In 1779, the infantry lieutenant and engineer Don Dionisio Baldenoche saw the dog that could make itself invisible, and in 1801 the mayor of Matanzas, Don Ignacio de Lamar, saw it. The first governor of Matanzas, Brigadier Don Juan Tirry, also saw it in 1815.

But all these witnesses to the invisible and apparently eternal life of the dog with the lunar coat and luminous blue eyes, when asked about it, played down their respective encounters with the invisible dog of Matanzas. They simply maintained that perhaps they each had seen a shadow on the night of the full moon, which they had mistaken for a dog. And the invisible dog of Matanzas became an established tradition.

In Europe, in Nice, a man from Matanzas, Alejandro Odero (born in 1827), painted the Invisible Dog of Matanzas. The painting with such an absurd theme was lost in later years.

In February 1863, the poet José Jacinto Milanés y Fuentes claimed that he knew of the invisible dog and that it was almost always the solace of the lonely, the friend of artists and poets, and the faithful protector of the immortal soul of the city of Matanzas. The national poet, Bonifacio Byrne, wrote a sonnet to the invisible dog. Had he seen it? No one knows.

The invisible dog carries on its mysterious mission in the streets of Matanzas. Those who can see it know that it is the very same dog that Doña Ramonita Oramas, the widow of Solís, described on her deathbed in the barely remembered year of 1771.

Scarface

The sun was setting gently and peacefully. Its golden disk rested on the spectacular colors of the distant horizon. In the dreamlike twinkling of the last light of the evening, the dark silhouette of a carriage was reflected on the stony, muddy surface of the street, moving like a gloomy shadow that portends misfortune and sorrow. That imposing and elegant coach was drawn by a fine team of black-maned horses. Their gentle, rhythmic trotting echoed in the silence of the narrow street.

The vehicle finally stopped in front of a large house with wide doors and discolored, dirty windows. Also dirty was the canopy that attempted to protect the worn, mossy flags of the pavement from the rain and the sun. A man, elegantly and formally dressed, as was the fashion among doctors of medicine of the day, stepped down majestically from the carriage. The man was handsome and he had a distinguished air, but there was something mysterious and sinister about his reddish gaze.

Stroking his mouth and chin, covered by a narrow moustache and a pointed beard, the strange individual knocked gently on the creaking door. It opened slowly to reveal the figure of a pale, sad woman inside.

"Can I help you, sir?"

"I am the doctor," replied the strange visitor, "and I would like to see the patient."

The figure of the woman moved slowly aside. In the dim light of a gas lamp, she looked like an elderly woman on whose wrinkled face life's suffering had left indelible traces. It seemed as if she bore the weight of a century on her stooped shoulders, suffering the burden of the illness of the man whom the doctor had come to see.

"This way," said the woman, leading the doctor to a sparsely furnished bedroom in the middle of which the patient rested in a badly made bed.

The doctor, who never stopped stroking his fine, well-kept beard, said gravely: "Leave me alone with the patient for a moment." He closed the door and, fixing his cold, piercing gaze on the sick man, examined him thoroughly.

The man who lay there looked about sixty but well preserved. He had a fierce gaze, and the evil hidden in his heart was reflected in his face. A huge scar ran from the right side of his forehead down to his beard, horribly disfiguring his face.

When the doctor's eyes came to rest on the sick man, he exclaimed: "Scarface!"

The sick man opened his eyes and asked: "Who are you?"

At that precise moment, the doctor, whose eyes and face took on a reddish hue and from whose forehead two horns sprouted, replied with a sarcastic smile: "You don't recognize me? I am the Devil, and I have come for your soul, for your cruel soul that beat your children and tormented your wife." Then, taking in his paws the face of the sick man, who was seized by terror, he clawed at it until it began to bleed copiously. The man's eyes popped in fright,

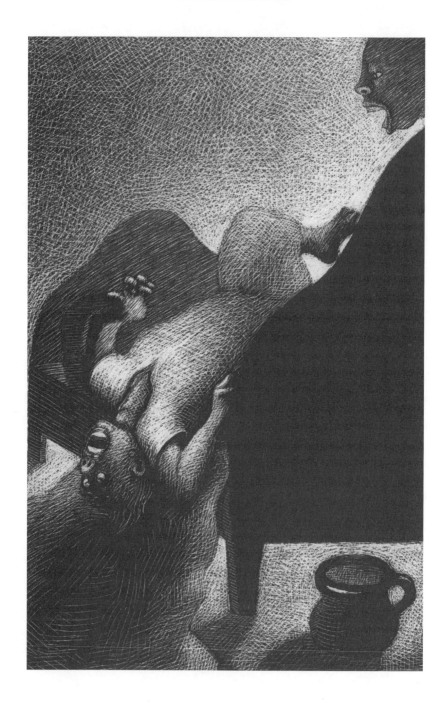

and his mouth contracted into a rictus of death. He was a corpse!

In the stony and damp street a cloud covered the spot where the coach had stood.

When she heard her husband's desperate cries, the woman opened the door of the room and gazed on the horrific scene: in the bed lay the twisted body of Scarface. Recovering from the shock, she searched for the doctor, but doctor and carriage had disappeared without anyone seeing them.

So it was that in the Camagüey of long ago, this legend was told by our grandmothers fearfully and furtively as they remembered what they had so often heard, that the Devil had taken Scarface's evil soul away!

The White Vulture

In the land I love, irrigated by the crystal, resonant waters of the shady Tínima, on the fertile plains of the heart of the Queen of the Antilles, lies the noble city of Puerto Principe, that it pleased Heaven to make my home. In the far-off times of my childhood there lived a venerable monk of the Franciscan Order, whom everyone familiarly called Father Valencia, for it was known that he had been born by the banks of the Turia.

That man was loved by everyone throughout the land. This was as it should be, for in the many years he had spent there not a day had gone by when he did not generously spread his services and blessings among its inhabitants.

If the domestic peace and harmony within a certain family was upset, the respected Father Valencia would appear as if sent by the hand of God. The wise advice, paternal exhortations, and affectionate entreaties spoken by that gentle voice would soon restore peace and harmony.

If a conflict of interests or opinion provoked bloody discord between neighbors and threatened ill will and revenge, the peace-loving Father would immediately go to mediate the struggle. The powerful influence of that evangelical spirit, conciliatory and loving, soothed irate passions as if by magic, and he always found a means of reaching compromise and agreement.

If the scandalous excesses of some public sinner outraged prudish consciences, perhaps threatening the preservation of respectable habits, Father Valencia would soon find delicate and ingenious ways of establishing friendly communications with the person who was causing the problem. Not much time would go by without the contact with a life of such great purity transforming the licentiousness into exercises of austere penitence.

If those of noble or common birth, rich or poor, were affected by some irreparable loss or cruel misfortune, Father Valencia always hastened to add his tears to those of the suffering. The balm of his consoling words effectively healed the deepest wounds of the heart.

In a word, that humble friar became providence manifest for the whole town. There, the immense tenderness of his soul and the unending supply of his Christian charity never failed to seek and find a remedy or at least relief, for any dispute, whether public or private.

However, there was one terrible affliction, whose sad spectacle could be seen at every turn, without the holy man being able to solve it. Lepers wandered through the streets, spoiling the atmosphere with the stench of their sores, begging alms for the love of God that even the most pious could not give without averting their eyes from their revolting appearance. These wretched creatures, a hazard to public health, were increasing in number every day, even though many died. They lived packed together in humble and filthy hovels that medical science never reached to give them relief. Even the ministers of religion did not always go there to offer them the last rites in their dying moments.

Only Father Valencia discovered and frequented these reposito-
ries of poverty, these sources of infection, delighting in the difficult care of such revolting patients. But he well knew that all his
self-denial could not insure the resources and comforts they so
badly needed. This disheartening thought troubled him greatly
until the day dawned when, suddenly enlightened by divine inspi-
ration, he threw a beggar's bag across his shoulder and began to
travel around the city. He went from door to door asking for a few
coins to found a big leper hospital.

One might laugh at such an apparently futile undertaking. How
could one imagine it would be possible to collect from public charity sufficient funds to build and maintain such an important institution in a city that lacked significant sources of wealth?

According to the law of common sense such a hope was truly
absurd, but according to Father Valencia's faith, it seemed possible
and, sure enough, it became a reality. It only took a few years to
build up from the foundations the vast and fine building that is a
tribute to his memory in the city of Camagüey. Hundreds of sick
people of both sexes were welcomed into it, to general approval.
They found in that isolated and healthy refuge run by its honorable
founder all the comforts and even pleasures their situation required. The blessings of heaven that constantly accompanied the
commendable Franciscan made the model hospital, of which
Puerto Principe was so proud, more successful each day during the
time he was in charge of it.

But the day eventually came when the father of the wretched
lepers was called to happier regions where the reward for his heroic virtues awaited him. His absence was soon sorely felt, despite
the determination of the good and generous inhabitants of the
region to endeavor to prevent the decline of that institution, which

was especially needed in a place where elephantiasis and the like spread periodically in an alarming fashion.

But the serious problems really began in the year when, through a fatal combination of circumstances that need not be detailed here, there was severe hardship and deprivation throughout the whole central province of Cuba. Then gangs of starving beggars could be seen swarming through the streets. The members of the well-off classes, whom they asked for money, were also affected by the crises going on throughout the land. They did not have the bottomless supply of alms needed to satisfy the hunger of the destitute mob. As one might have foreseen, the leper hospital suffered greatly from the state of general poverty.

Accustomed to abundance and the comforts their provident founder had managed to find for them, the inmates suffered the many deprivations it was necessary to impose. These increased daily until they feared they might have to leave the shelter of the hospital where they had hoped to see out their sorry existence in peace.

Faced with this terrible dilemma, they went tearfully to the modest grave where the ashes of their unforgettable benefactor were buried. They called fervently on his blessed spirit to help them from heaven, where they did not doubt he now lived.

Nevertheless, the hardships increased. The hospital administration had exhausted all their energy and intelligence. They no longer knew how to go on maintaining the many patients, whose complaints and lamentations intensified the unhappiness of their spirits in the face of such insurmountable difficulties.

One morning at around twelve, the poor lepers had not yet been able to breakfast. They lay sadly on the grass that grew in the orchard of the establishment, now ruined. They tearfully recalled

the time when flocks of colorful tropical songbirds used to come
to the trees each morning to peck at the abundant leftovers of the
breakfast food. "Ay!" they said. "Now only carnivorous vultures
come here as if waiting to gorge themselves on our dead bodies."

And indeed a great many of these foul and somber birds that I
recall used to arouse a superstitious dread when I was a girl, could
be seen moving slowly and carefully around the orchard. The buzzard, or great Cuban vulture, as you may perhaps know, dear reader, is undoubtedly one of the rare exceptions among the numerous
species of beautiful indigenous birds. Its head, a purplish red, has
scabby excrescences, which is why it is called tiñosa.[1] Its curved
beak and sharp claws, tinged blood red like the rest of its body,
emit the fetid odor of the putrid flesh that is its habitual nourish-
ment. When its wings, a dull greenish black, beat the air, they
make a sinister murmuring sound that seems to mark a funereal
rhythm.

However, on the day in question, while the hospital's inmates
were unhappily watching the somber procession that accompanied
their solitude, making it even more gloomy, a strange bird suddenly appeared among the dark and sinister flock. It was the same
size and shape as the vultures but contrasted with them in an amaz-
ing way. It was as white as the swan; its head, feet, and beak were
rose-colored; and instead of the shifty eyes of the species to which
it seemed to belong, it had the sweet and melancholy eyes of the
wood pigeon.

The lepers, amazed to see such a new and unexpected apparition, approached it curiously, and a strange thing happened; the
flock of black vultures immediately flew away as if frightened.
The white vulture did not flee but meekly allowed itself to be
caught and even seemed to want to caress with its gently flapping

wings the ulcerous hands holding it.

The following day, this moving tale spread throughout Puerto Principe. It was said that Father Valencia's soul, so often invoked in their growing anguish by his poor children, the lepers, had come down among them in the form of an extraordinary bird that everyone called the "white vulture." The news of the incident awoke so much interest that a public display of the bird had to be arranged. An entry fee was charged, and so many people came that within a few days a considerable sum was collected, enough to meet the urgent needs of the St. Lazarus hospital.

But it did not end there. The "white vulture" was paraded in a golden cage in many Cuban towns, arousing keen interest everywhere. It raised voluntary contributions for the establishment and enabled it to finally emerge from its difficulties and enter a new phase of prosperity and comfort.

According to popular belief, even after his death, the charitable founder had managed to provide for his inmates, who hailed the appearance of the "white vulture" as a visible miracle that confirmed the holiness and eternal bliss of that generous soul.

What became of the miraculous bird once its mission was accomplished? No one has been able to tell me for sure, however much I inquire. But if one day these jumbled pages are read by my dear compatriots, none will deny the truth of this event. I have chosen to include it in my legends as a mark of honor and respect for the venerable monk who so often blessed me in my early years, and in lasting memory of the beautiful land where my cradle rocked.

The House of Bones

It is unlikely that, at the time, the inhabitants of the incipient town of Santa Clara would have believed that, over the years, a street lighting system would appear that was an improvement on the pathetic, feeble one that existed then. This consisted of lanterns hung from iron hooks in the doorways of wealthy inhabitants. Each one held an oil lamp. The glass was blackened at the top by smoke and at the bottom misted over by the bad weather. The light only reached a few steps in its futile contest against the shadows.

The law of contrasts meant that, in the variable distance between lanterns, their negative capacity, which could only hope to mimic the effect of a red brushstroke on a dark canvas, actually intensified the shadows' somber hold. These were broken here and there by feeble strips of dim light escaping from the doors or windows of a house inside which burned the legendary tallow candle in a potbellied lamp.

The inhabitants were not night owls. They locked their doors at an early hour and devoted themselves quietly to their rest. On the nights, most of them, when there was no moon to assist in the municipality's task of lighting the streets of the town, the streets were a sight to be seen, especially when the nocturnal breeze, sneaking in between the gaps in a broken or rickety lantern here and there, extinguished a lamp and erased the red brushstrokes from the shadowy scene. Then the patch of darkness was unbroken. It inspired a certain fearful shrinking of the spirit in those who had to venture out in the night hours. Then the trees, whose branches spread over patio walls or the fences of the many areas of wasteland that bordered the street, appeared more solid and threatened to engulf it. This shrinking feeling was hardly surprising given that those good people were known to be superstitious and to believe in goblins and ghosts.

However, it had considerable advantages for gamblers and suitors. For the former it made it easier to outwit the vigilance of authority and to meet in arranged venues to fleece one another without bumping into constables or the long arm of the law. It afforded the latter opportunities for courting the lady of their choice, beyond the reach of prying eyes or untrustworthy ears. It even enabled them to bring to a successful conclusion some adventure in which an unwelcome witness would be an insurmountable obstacle.

And we are not referring to those with time on their hands, who dedicate themselves to meddling in other people's affairs. Fortunately such people were rare in the town. Those were the good old days of unquestionable honesty and honorable, almost patriarchal ways, when other people's property was respected just as much as it is coveted today.

There was a house on Luis Estévez Street, formerly known as St. John the Baptist Street, but more commonly as the Street of the Little Bones, perhaps on account of the event that we are going to relate. It was very close to the main square, then in its early stages. There lived a girl whom we shall call Mercedes so as to avoid any recriminations from some distant descendant. But we will say is that she was strikingly pretty, like a spring flower. She was twenty years old, and her voice, smile, and grace enhanced the blessings of her youth. She was the daughter of the ordinary mayor of the town. We use the word "ordinary" to precisely denote his post, for that was his title, rather than to allude to his extreme brusqueness, his rustic nature, his unfriendly appearance and his tendency to fly into a rage at the first sign of trouble. It must be said, with all due respect to his role as ordinary mayor of the town and also as father of the lovely Mercedes, that this quality frequently made him look a fool.

This attractive woman was courted by a sturdy, well-groomed, likeable, and witty youth. He had all the qualities needed to win the heart of that girl and others of a more elevated social position than the one to whom he was engaged. Although the girl was extremely fond of him, the youth did not know how to insure her father's consent nor how to even attempt to win it with any hope of success.

For the time being, he had her affection. She allowed him to love her, and she loved him in return, and he had something more: the promise that she would appear before the shutter of her bedroom window in the early hours of the morning when her parents and neighbors had already retired. This was their only means of communication. Even so it ran the risk of being curtailed if it came to the mayor's notice, if not because he was the mayor, then because he was a father.

On the night when our enamored youth attempted to employ this recourse for the first time, he went very quietly up to his beloved's window. He was about to give the prearranged knock when he noticed the lantern in the doorway of that house, which had to be present in the house of the leading authority of the town to set an example. It illuminated the spot to such an extent that anyone standing beside the window could be seen from a distance.

Without hesitating, he climbed the lamppost. Thanks to his height and the mighty puff he aimed at the oil lamp, he immediately extinguished the light.

But there was another problem. The house opposite had a window shielded by curved wooden balusters, many of which were missing. Behind this, through a shutter that was open despite the late hour, a faint light could be seen inside. The indistinct silhouette of a woman could be seen, and by all appearances, she was watching what went on in the street.

The young man hesitated. Had the mayor stationed someone there to keep an eye on his house? He decided to confront the prying woman—there was no doubt it was a woman—and ask her why she was spying on other people's affairs. But, wishing to attain his goal by a sure path rather than ruin everything in a moment of impatience, he held back so as not to reveal himself and finally decided to go away.

Three or four times on successive nights he tried to approach Mercedes's window, which was becoming the door to purgatory when he had been promised entry into heaven. Each time he saw the aforementioned silhouette of the woman behind that indiscreet shutter.

"I will have to scare this good-for-nothing old woman," he said. "Who can it be?" He was furious. For all that time he had been unable to exchange a single word with Mercedes. He thought that the girl would believe his intentions were not serious or that he was afraid to call her through the window. The injury done to his image as a devoted lover and to his courage made him ready to do something mischievous, were it not that she would be the first to suffer the consequences.

The particulars we have of the woman who was thwarting our lovers' plans suggest that, for her part, she really had no such intention. She was a pious old woman, as sleepless as an owl, who lived with an old African woman. She sat behind the window to get the breeze from the street, until midnight, when she went to bed.

As she was old, pious, and a night owl, this naturally leads us to suppose that she was a busybody. Although it is not known whether the mayor assigned her to watch his house, no sooner had it got dark then she would be looking out of her window waiting for the Holy Rosary to go past. As soon as this happened, she remained at her observation post. This was partly to get some fresh air and kill time and partly to observe those who were out late, whether one door was opened or another closed, and so on. She was stocking up on material for the following day's gossip with others of her ilk and interests. It has been suggested that she was peeping out to see whether it were true that witches go silently at an unearthly hour to meet in their coven. But such an assertion is probably slanderous.

Before we proceed, let us point out that one of the many religious practices and customs of true believers of the time was to organize night processions in the churches. The faithful of all ages, sexes, and rank, with the priest and the sacristan at the head of the procession, went through the streets with lighted candles, praying the rosary. Then they would return to the church. These nocturnal peregrinations ended on the day of Our Lady of the Rosary, when there was a big religious celebration. Those inhabitants who did not join these nocturnal processions watched them from the doorways of their houses, praying fervently and with recollection as they passed. This is what the old neighbor of the mayor used to do.

When Mercedes's lover had given up hoping that the impertinent witness would leave the field open, he became a regular churchgoer in order to take part in the Rosary Procession. When passing the house of the old hag—as he so rudely called her—he lingered in order to watch it and check its interior so as to find out who lived there and any other useful information. He took the precaution of wearing different clothes each time, turning up the collar of his jacket or turning down his hat so as not to be recognized.

At other times, he changed his clothing and made the round after the Rosary. He was certain that only the two women lived in the house and that the one who stayed at the window was always the same one, the pious old woman. On one of these rounds, ready now to try out a plan of action he had devised, he very quietly went up to the window. He looked up and down the street and, not seeing a living soul, jumped up noisily, held on to the balusters for a few seconds, and then ran away at top speed.

The old woman let out a "Jesus help me!" Trembling with fright, she slammed the shutter to. The mischievous youth heard the cry and, looking back, saw the closed shutter. But he did not want to approach that of his beloved, as he feared startled neighbors might open theirs to see what had happened. If it were true that the night owl waited for witches, she now had something to convince her.

The next night, as soon as the Holy Rosary had passed with the young man in the procession as usual, he could see that the old woman had closed the shutter and that the house was quiet.

"This is going well," he thought. But, when he returned two hours later, as before, he was annoyed to see that the shutter was, if not open, then ajar, and behind the opening was the same face which he recognized in the semidarkness.

He then went home quickly, put on a long overcoat, pulled his hat down over his eyes. Placing under his arm a strange bundle that he took from a drawer, he returned to the house of his nightmares. He stopped in front of the said window with an enigmatic gesture. At that moment, the shutter closed as if by magic. He tapped on the wood and, deepening his voice, said: "Good woman, look after this for me."

No one answered, and he repeated: "Look after this for me, in the name of the Virgin."

The shutter gradually opened halfway, and from within a nasal voice inquired: "What am I to look after?"

"This, a couple of candles and a candlestick," he said, shoving the package through the gap left by a fallen baluster, not giving the old woman time to close the shutter. She took the package, trembling and reluctant, while the youth added: "Tomorrow and each night I will bring you more until the house is full." And he went away quickly, making hardly any noise and without letting her see his face during that brief conversation. The face one should have seen was that of the old woman when, having turned the strange package over and over and felt it on the outside, she decided to unwrap it to see the candles and candlestick she thought were inside. Instead she found two tibias and a skull. She remembered the stranger's promise that he would bring her more on the following nights until her house was filled.

Tradition does not tell, nor is it known how the inveterate night owl spent the night, on that occasion definitely sleepless. What is known is that shortly after dawn the next day she went out to look for a house to move into. She did so that morning. The undertaking was watched from a nearby spot by Mercedes's lover, laughing to himself crazily and rubbing his hands in glee.

That same night and following the aforementioned blowing out of the lamp at the mayor's house, the two lovers began the agreed means of communication through a shutter that was more discreet than that of the house opposite. It remained unlet as the rumor quickly spread that it was uninhabitable because goblins or witches came at night to store human bones, which there was no point in refusing as they could make them pass through walls and partitions.

Revenge

Tradition does not reveal the names of the characters in the drama that was so famous in its day. Naturally, it was known who they were, and the event was much talked-about at the time and in the years that followed. But so many have gone by—more than a century—that not only is it no longer known who they were, but it is a long time since parents recounted the event to their children at moments deemed appropriate. Sometimes they claimed it was a true story, other times an imaginary event. However, it should be pointed out that it was actually the former, that is, true and real though, as happens in such cases, the particulars, motives, and other circumstances varied. This is because it was handed down by tradition and over time details tend to be altered.

How and why the two men began to hate each other remains a mystery and has always been a point of conjecture. It is true that one of them hated the other more intensely and more wholeheartedly. Possibly the other man had almost forgotten the quarrel, or at least he no longer attached any importance to it and carried on as normal.

The other man was different. He conceived the idea of revenge and began coldly and calculatingly to plan ways of achieving it with the least risk to his person and the greatest chance of success.

When he had devised a plan, he moved to Puerto Principe. This gave some degree of respite to those most involved in the event— the quarrel between the two men. Especially the man who stayed behind in the small town, confident now that with his enemy gone, things would be unlikely to get out of hand.

He would not have felt thus had he known of the ideas and schemes of the other man. Living now in Puerto Principe, he began to lead an active life, as he was apparently not short of means. He embarked on business ventures and got to know many people. This was all part of his plan.

His business required him to travel out of the city frequently and to spend several days away. He used these absences to further his main plan: revenge. All along the road from that city to this, he left horses carefully chosen for their stamina. They were spread conveniently between farms adjoining the road so as not to attract attention, with the promise that he would come back and collect them as soon as his business pursuits allowed.

He planned to make his proposed visit to Santa Clara but to spend as short a time as possible away from Puerto Principe, so that if there was an inquiry, everyone would agree that they had not noticed his absence. If all else failed, he was in any case always going away, never for more than four or five days, during which time it would be impossible to travel to Santa Clara and back.

When he had everything ready, he left at around ten at night. Not sparing the horses, as the saying goes, he changed his mount at each of the places where he had previously left a spare. Covering the distance at a gallop, he reached Santa Clara on the third day. He left his mount at the inn stable and wrapped himself in a large cloak beneath which he concealed a long-barreled firearm.

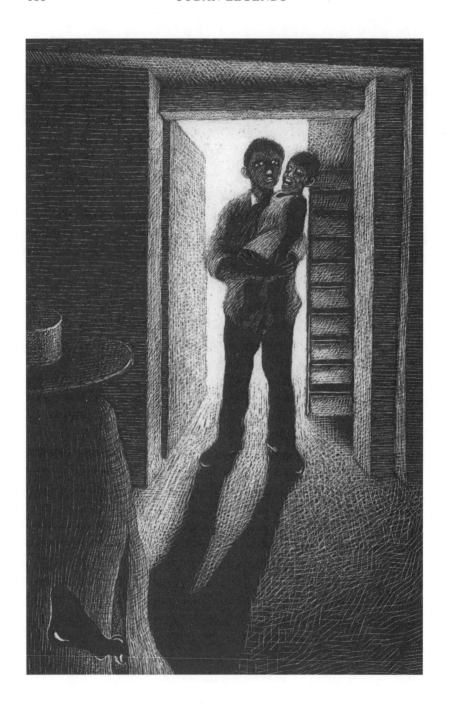

He went toward San Cristobal Street, between San José and Sancti Spiritus. He headed for the barren piece of wasteland opposite his rival's house and waited. It was late afternoon on a rainy day, which made the cloak seem appropriate.

Soon the man he was looking for came to the door, but he was carrying in his arms a little girl, possibly his daughter. Thus he waited patiently. Shortly afterward the man went inside, left the child, and came back into the doorway in a casual manner, like someone who has nothing to fear. Although it was getting dark, his silhouette was clearly framed in the doorway. The cloaked man did not wait any longer; he fired and watched as the victim of the shooting toppled over.

He flung his still-smoking gun to the ground and escaped through the back streets, cautiously at first and then more quickly. He reached the inn where he had left his horse, paid the fee, and swiftly headed for the road back to Puerto Principe, intending to use the same strategy as when he had come; that is, ride at full gallop, changing horses along the way. In three days or less he would be home, and no one would remark on his absence, which would be less than five days in total.

But the lucky star that seemed thus far to guide him was eclipsed. Around ten at night, pitch black on account of the inclement weather, taking a shortcut through the area around the Buenviaje hermitage, then and for many years after unlit wasteland, he fell into an unmarked well. He was lifted out early the next morning by some inhabitants who thought they could hear voices crying for help and went to see where they were coming from.

What happened next has not passed down to our days. The tradition breaks off at this point. Except that, some years later, the figure of the murderer, a man wrapped in a cloak with the barrel of a gun poking from its folds, was on display in the city's first wax museum. This was located in the house that became the Ferrolana Inn, later demolished to make way for the Santa Clara hotel. Verses by an unknown author printed on loose sheets also circulated. These told more or less the same story as that recounted here and lamented the avenger's misfortune.

Apart from the verses, we are not aware that anything else has been written about this event, which was kept alive by tradition in provincial circles for God knows how many years until, as with all our traditions, it vanished completely.

The Witches

Witches are found everywhere, or this was so when they used to wander around the world. Nowadays they rarely allow themselves to be seen in a remote corner of some country slowly reached by progress, which has proved more powerful than they since it has compelled them to fly away, God knows where. We shall not follow them to wherever that may be as it is those of our native land that interest us.

In Cuba there used to be witches, quite a few, if we believe the traditions, though it is unclear whether they were indigenous or whether they were brought by the Spaniards who colonized and ruled the country or by black Africans who suffered the burden of colonization from below. The fact is, witches existed, or if one is to be truthful, there were many people who believed in their existence and others who boasted they had seen them. This is why the popular imagination has collected and spread tales about these old women with big noses who usually appear riding on a broomstick.

Here are some cases gathered at random. One night a farmer left this city or growing town for his nearby home on the road to Granadillo. He went on foot, and, as he was passing through a marshy ravine, looking for the best place to cross the swamp, he felt himself seized from behind, hoisted into the air and thrown onto the opposite bank to the cry of: "Mother Marota; there goes the ball!"

He might have been pleased to have crossed the swamp without getting dirty, but, before he realized what had happened or what would come next, he was caught on the other side and thrown back to the opposite bank, to the same cry of: "Mother Marota, there goes the ball!"

No one knows how that game of catch ended, for this is all that is known or has been told of the mishap of the farmer who was thrown back and forth by witches.

Another night, two horsemen trotting in opposite directions through a narrow alley in San Gil found themselves in a wide swamp, one of the many found on our rural roads—there are still quite a few today. There was only one place where it was possible to pass without the danger of ones mount getting badly stuck in the mud or of falling in, horse and all.

They both held back and waited for the other to begin crossing, or they both began to cross at the same time. After a moment, they did the same again with the same result, as if their movements were synchronized. It seemed this would go on forever until one of the horsemen, no doubt the most resolute, said to the other: "Friend, either you go first or I will."

He did not need to repeat the suggestion. The horseman on the opposite bank turned into a horsewoman, and her mount turned into a broomstick, and they rose into the air, leaving the way clear for the other traveler. Afterward he told anyone who would listen what had happened, swearing that it was true, "cross my heart!"

Another appearance by these ladies of the midnight apparel took place in broad daylight in a remote rural area of this district.

It was eleven o'clock in the morning on a windy day in March when, carried at a great height by a gust of wind, a sheet, a long piece of rope, and even more unusually, a wooden club, went flying by.

Two brothers from Asturias who fervently believed in witches, either because they discovered their existence here or because they also appear in Asturias, knew at once what was happening, unlike some peasants who were gazing at the sight, thinking, for want of a better explanation, that it was caused by the strong wind, though this could not explain the flying club. One of the brothers, who also knew the countermeasures to be applied in such cases, drove a machete into the ground, a magic spell to make them fall and lose all their magic power.

All those present saw how the sheet, the rope, and the bar swiftly fell to earth. When the most resolute, preceded by the man with the machete, ran to where the objects had appeared to fall, they found only a few ashes. This merely confirmed what they had said about it being genuine witches, who on this occasion had dared to come out during the daytime, albeit disguised in quite an unusual manner, as we have described.

There was a time when half the population believed in the existence of witches, and many stories and accounts of their appearance circulated and this or that place where they had been seen was pointed out. This happened even in other countries with more ancient civilizations, for one must acknowledge that they were once to be found everywhere. But there as here, the railway, electricity, and other signs of progress have made them disappear.

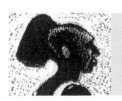

The Widows

The widows who were so common—and even somewhat feared —for a number of years in Santa Clara, vanished from our scene, gradually at first and then more completely. The War of Independence did away with them as the exodus of patriots, the death of many, and the placing of peasants in concentration camps brought about many radical changes in our habits and customs. It is not possible to specify the date of their first appearance, but we can confirm that, for a time, they were thought to be ghosts, until knowledge of their habits and customs made it possible to classify them properly.

The reader will of course have realized that we are not referring to the women who have lost their husbands, for these exist and will continue to do so as long as the institution of marriage lasts. It is the other "widows," who in times long past frequently frightened the neighbors.

We do not know if they were found in other Cuban towns, but we tend to think they were. They served the purpose for which they were invented, and we feel sure that they must have spread from here to other places or were imported from elsewhere into this region.

At their peak, three nights in a row would not go by without someone saying that "a widow appeared" in some alleyway or piece of waste ground. More than one sleepless inhabitant would see through her shutters one passing swiftly by. They were always wrapped in long black dresses, hence the name widows. Their faces were covered, and they avoided indiscreet glances. They were not thieves, at least not of material things, though it cannot be said that they did not steal other people's honor.

At that time there were many pieces of wasteland, some open, some fenced in on the street side by stunted pines or rickety boards that allowed a stealthy widow to pass through without needing to have recourse to the railing or balcony mentioned in Zeno Gandía's monumental verse "La Palmada."

Nor was it a question of a local Don Juan having to break into a convent to abduct a Doña Inés, for the simple reason that there were no convents. There were certainly Don Juans, but homespun Tenorios who made a prior appointment to enter someone else's home with sinful intentions. The main thing they had to avoid was possible witnesses, talkative neighbors, or even another suitor who might be involved in the same or similar activities. They were not the same as ghosts that disappeared when they were discovered, as we mentioned earlier. If some nervous old woman crossed herself when she saw one or knew it was prowling round the neighborhood, it was because there was always some degree of doubt as to whether they were what most believed them to be, or some tormented soul that had assumed human form.

As time went by everything would come out. If they never managed to discover the names of the lady who had given rise to the apparition and the person who was the "widow" of the moment, they came close, very close. As night follows day, the house would

be discovered. Only in a few cases would it be necessary to deter-
mine which of the ladies living in the house—if there was more
than one with the qualities necessary to arouse suspicion—should
take the blame.

On one occasion, two widows who were going about their business met in an out-of-the-way alley. They were mutually incom-
patible; that is, each one went in the opposite direction so that she,
or rather he, would not to be found out.

Otherwise, these widows became so plentiful that three or four
could be seen on any night in different parts of the city, providing
ample material for rumor and gossip. It is not that we are calling
into question the virtue of the ladies of the time. Instead, what is
done quite shamelessly today, in those days they attempted wherever possible to preserve if not decorum, then its appearance. Thus
the widows were invented who were not widows at all, but real
men going about their business.

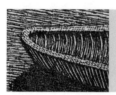

The Appearance
of the Virgin of Charity
# of El Cobre

At the beginning of the seventeenth century, when the town of the Mine of El Cobre was founded by His Catholic Majesty, it so happened that three men set out from the hato² of Barajagua, near to the said town, to collect salt in the Bay of Nipe. Two of them were native Indians; one was called Rodrigo de Joyos and the other Juan de Joyos. The brothers were accompanied by a third person, a black Creole from the same town called Juan Moreno, who would have been around nine or ten. It was he who, at the age of seventy or seventy-one, gave the best eyewitness account of the vision. When they reached the said Bay of Nipe, the three stayed at a place called Cayo Francés or la Vigía.

They remained there on the day of their arrival. The following day they attempted to set out for the coast in a canoe to collect the salt but were unable to do so on account of the high winds and rough sea. Nor could they begin their journey on the following day as the weather was still bad. The delay upset them a great deal. But by the end of the third day, seeing that, from midnight as the fourth day was beginning, the sea was calm and the weather settled, they attempted to begin their journey. As the weather looked favorable, they set off in the early morning, hoping to arrive safely.

Thus they began to row. When they had gone some distance from the Vigía, it began to get light. The sea was calm, and in the misty light the three seafarers could made out in the distance a white shape like those birds that fly with their wings almost touching the waves. Seeing this strange sight, they leaned on their oars and headed toward the shape that was going in the same direction. Now as the day grew lighter and the vision came closer, they saw that what looked like a bird was the statue of Holy Mary, hail full of grace, that appeared to be flying toward them. Seeing this wonder, they brought the canoe closer. Taking the statue in their hands, they put it inside. In the statue's left hand was a lovely child and in her right, a golden cross.

They were entranced by what they had seen and more so when they noticed that it had come on a small plank that served as the boat on which it sailed calmly and smoothly without even getting her dress wet. Determined now to continue their journey, they stopped when they saw some large letters written on the small plank that they had left behind on the sea and that was coming nearer. They took this with them as well, and Rodrigo de Joyas, who could read, saw that the letters said: I AM THE VIRGIN OF CHARITY.

Taking this much-traveled treasure and also the said plank, they at last resumed their journey to the salt pan. When they reached it they collected three packs of salt . They made the packs from the leaf of one of the palm trees of this island that is called the yagua or royal palm. Well supplied now with what they had come for, they began their return journey to the Vigia. They were happy, not so much because they had got what they came for but because they were carrying with them such a precious a treasure, Our Lady that they had found on the sea.

When they reached land, after drawing up and securing the canoe, they honored the divine statue, placing it as decently as possible in one of the bunks or barbacoas on which the natives take their rest, while they quickly prepared to take their divine discovery back to the hato of Barajagua, more than fifteen leagues from Vigía. It was a few more leagues from the hato of Barajagua to the Royal Mines of El Cobre where the statue was finally taken.

The Dead Man's Cave

Over a century ago, four and a half leagues from Cárdenas on the road to Matanzas, by the coast and in the shelter of steep hills, stood a group of thatched bohíos inhabited mainly by grimy coal miners. Later, sugar mills would cover the vast plain that looks towards the sea, and that tiny village would become the thriving and prosperous town of Camarioca.

But at the dawn of the nineteenth century, anyone traveling along that rugged coastline and through those uncultivated fields that were turned into vast marshes by the flooding of the Camarioca and Canímar Rivers, could easily imagine themselves on a desert island not reached even by the faintest echo of Cuban life.

When the north wind blew during our short, mild winter that is a benevolent imitation of the harsh season in cold countries, the waves crashed, exploding with foam from Maya Point as far as the entrance to the little port. They traced a garland of snow along the green bends of the coast that was adorned with natural beauty like a beautiful, naked virgin.

No living soul had ever been seen on the deserted and silent coast. By day, the saramagullón, seagull, and huge gannet with its enormous beak enlivened the solitude with their cries. When night fell, the silence was broken by the guttural, piercing cry of the sijú,[3] the siguapa,[4] and the owl. The luxuriant tropical vegetation rose like a curtain between the impoverished community and the coast. Wild vines climbed over the dense plantation bushes and guacamaya.[5]

The exact year is not known, but it was at the beginning of the Age of Enlightenment, as has been mentioned. Some country folk, perhaps those who marked the path that is today the road from the shanty town to Varadero beach, were climbing down through the rocks of the narrow defile when they discovered a cave, not very deep, as light from outside reached to the back. A terrible sight made them emerge hastily. In the middle of the cave they saw a bare skeleton. It was lying covered in a priest's habit and holding an open breviary in its bony, rigid hands.

Word of the somber discovery spread quickly throughout the little community, where events of such importance never occurred. The more or less straightforward account of the find raised murmurs in all those little houses made of palm leaves. The initial horrified reaction was soon followed by an overwhelming curiosity that led the bravest to the Cave of the Dead. In the presence of those remains of someone completely unknown, whose posture suggested the untroubled and peaceful passing of one who had said his final farewell to life without the slightest fear of death, our normally superstitious peasants were overcome by noble thoughts. Instead of feeling afraid they prostrated themselves before the recumbent remains, believing them to be the relics of a blessed person who had in this world certainly been another "Holy Father" of Guanabacoa or another Father Valencia, the apostle of Puerto Príncipe, superhuman beings who left a radiant wake of admiration in souls and a true sentiment of love in people's hearts.

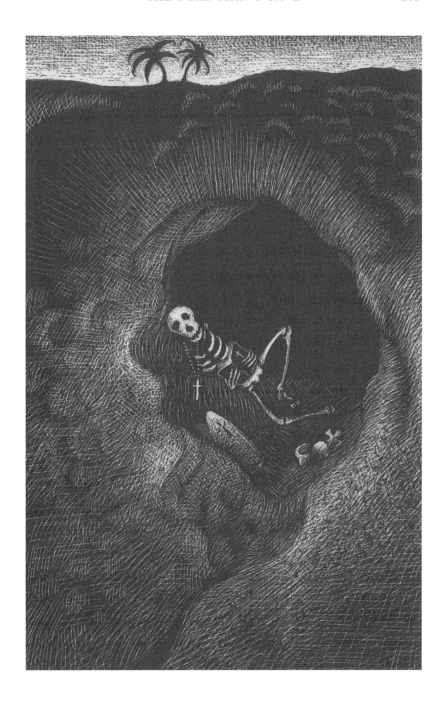

Who could that priest be, unknown anchorite of a new Thebaid,[6] whom no one had ever seen and whose death had passed unnoticed by all? Some thought he must have been a great sinner, perhaps a criminal who, repenting of his crimes, went to do penance in solitude, punishing his unruly flesh while his spirit spread its wings toward perfection. Others claimed he was simply a missionary who was suddenly taken ill on his travels. Unable to climb up to the shanty town in search of help, he had died in that place encountered providentially in his moment of affliction to shield him from the burning rays of the sun. But this version was less popular as simple souls are more easily convinced by the improbable. The person must have been a saint and should be worshiped and honored as a holy man.

The Fierce Indian

At the beginning of the nineteenth century, mid way through the year 1800, terror reigned in Puerto Príncipe and environs. Both the inhabitants of the island's second city and the peasants in the surrounding area were seized with a terrible panic. When the call to prayer rang out, they shut themselves in their stone and mud dwellings and did not even open the door to pay respect to the Sacrament.

To be quite fair to the people of Camagüey who had shown such bravery during the pirate incursions, we should point out that the panic began among the mothers whose most precious darlings were threatened: their children of tender age. It is not known where he came from, but a descendant of Hatuey appeared in the district. He was a full-blooded Indian, a stranger in his own land. In the Age of Enlightenment he was the anachronistic representative of a race that had almost completely died out by the mid-sixteenth century. Thus one may logically deduce that there were not many left at the time when our story took place.

He was a solitary descendant of the ill-fated Siboneys, decimated first by the barbarity of the Conquest and then by suicide, a desperate solution to their cruel suffering. For a wretched Indian,

alone, defenseless and completely naked, his only arms his club
and his spear, to be able to spread fear in a civilized society with
brave men and guns aplenty, other defensive or offensive resources
must have been operating in his favor. We will speak of this later.

The initial cry of alarm came from the first mother whose son
was taken away by the Fierce Indian, as he was known. This deed
made the people angry and later awakened the manly instinct
needed to avenge the crime that popular legend—whose fertile in-
ventiveness would be the envy of many novelists—embellished
with truly horrific events and circumstances.

The Fierce Indian, according to the vox populi, had the gift of
being everywhere at once, perhaps because his industry and dili-
gence enabled him to appear in different places at almost the same
time. He passed unseen through the streets of Puerto Príncipe. He
killed those who attempted to capture him and, employing unknown arts that gave him the reputation of magician and sorcerer,
snatched children and took them into the depths of the forest,
where they were never heard of again. Seemingly these innocent
creatures were a delicacy for the Indian who normally ate the
tongues of different animals. With extraordinary cruelty he would
cut out the tongue while they were still alive.

Of course, although one must accept the truth of some of what
was said and believed, tropical exaggeration, fear, and imagination
must also have added many pages to this remarkable legend.

According to Herrera, the Indians from Camagüey province
were renowned for their kind nature. They were hospitable, modest, simple, and shy. Among them anthropophagy was unknown.
Their food could not have been more primitive: cooked yucca,
corn meal, jutías, spiders, iguanas, fish, and cassava. Could such a
transformation in the tastes and pastimes of the last Siboney have

been possible?

As to his criminal activities, one could imagine that tradition, the recounting of the barbarities of the Conquest and the memories passed from fathers to sons of how Pánfilo de Narváez murdered the harmless natives of that same province, could awaken feelings of revenge in the Fierce Indian toward those who had exterminated his race.

Be that as it may, the town of Camagüey determined to defend itself against that dangerous visitor, who was in fact not a visitor but its original owner. Several groups of brave, armed townspeople rushed into the forest intending to capture or kill the murderous Indian.

In those days, Town Councils were an integral part of the town rather than a lot of politicos dedicated to gaining position at all costs. Eager to restore peace its residents, it allocated the sum of 500 pesos as a reward for whoever captured the Indian dead or alive. As we have already stated, this happened in 1800. In 1803 the child killer was still tormenting the people of Camagüey, and also the animals whose tongues he cut off with unheard-of cruelty. One sad event proved the last straw for the incensed townspeople. On the 10th of June of that year, one of Don José Matías Álvares's sons disappeared. The Fierce Indian had abducted him. Many people had seen him fleeing into the forest. Let us repeat: in those days the population did not remain calm as it does nowadays when brujos[7] abduct a child for their savage practices. No sooner was he abducted than a hundred men rushed after the Indian. Some going this way and others farther afield, they soon had him cornered. Fortunately they managed to rescue Álvares's son alive and unharmed, and the fearless townsmen, Don Agustín Arias and Don Serapio de Céspedes, also killed the kidnaper. They entered Puerto

Príncipe triumphantly at midnight, followed by a huge crowd, leading the body of their enemy thrown across a horse.

The people were so overjoyed that the bells of the ten or twelve churches in the city were rung at that hour to celebrate the happy event. There were many good things in the past be worth imitating in the newly established Republic.

Notes

Foreword
1. Barcelona: Editorial Destino, 1962.
2. Buenos Aires: Centro Editor de la América Latina, 1967, pp. 10–11.
3. Buenos Aires: Editorial Futuro, 1943.
4. Santiago de Chile: Editorial Universitaria, 1969.
5. Bohío, hut, shack.

Part One
1. Caucubú, golden stone.
2. Areíto, Popular songs and dances of the indigenous Cuban peoples.
3. Naridó, something that is red.
4. Guacabino, powerful brother.
5. Encomienda, a system that fixed Spanish conquistadors' entitlement to labor and tribute from the indigenous communities. It represented a form of slavery. Bartolomé de las Casas (1474–1566) renounced his encomienda and became the defender of Indian rights.
6. Behíque, medicine man.
7. Dujo, seat made from stone or a single piece of wood.
8. Jutía, ratlike mammal hunted for food.
9. Ecrara, seaside dwelling.
10. Caonareyto, golden verse.
11. Maguei, wind instrument.
12. Lambí, shell.
13. Nonum, the moon.
14. Boitio, priest.
15. Atabeira, mother of God.
16. Jagua, wild fruit from which a juice is extracted, used for body paint by the indigenous Cubans.
17. Turey, heaven.
18. Cemi, supernatural being or idol among the Taino Indians.
19. Ti, the earth.
20. Pitahaya, climbing plant with beautiful red flowers.
21. Guaní, hummingbird.

22. Cansí, hut inhabited by the chief.
23. Guatiní, climbing bird.
24. Cucubá, owl-like bird.
25. Guairo, small boat with two sails.
26. Guayacán, tree providing a strong, hard-wearing wood.
27. Caney, hut that is normally a chief's house.
28. Tocoloro, bird with multicolored plumage.
29. Tibisi, wild reed.
30. Dagame, tree with hard wood used for cart axles and other heavy carpentry.
31. Judío, bird common in Cuba.

Part Two

1. Babalao, babalawo, Ifá diviner.
2. Carabalí, name given in Spanish America to slaves from the Cross River region of present-day Nigeria and their language (from Calabar).
3. Cotunto, Antillean nocturnal bird of prey; pitirre, crested bird with an insistent and piercing song.
4. Ceiba, tree that is sacred to those who practice santería.
5. Omordé, woman.
6. Aché, sacred power.
7. Moquenquen, pl. moquenqueré, child.
8. Iyare, mother.
9. Osan-quiriñán, an avatar of Obatalá that is considered to be Olofi (the Supreme Deity) himself.
10. Ilé, house, dwelling.
11. Babá, name given to Obatalá in prayers and songs at the güemilere—party in honor of the orichas.
12. Achó, clothing, dress. (The order seems to have been reversed in the original text; see following note.)
13. Batá, shoes.
14. Amalá, Yoruba ritual food made from maize meal and mutton.
15. Iyá, here incorrectly used to mean "son"; it actually means "mother."
16. Oguedé, bananas.
17. Yalocha, daughter of the "saint." The male equivalent of this position in the santería hierarchy is babalocha.

18. Ekuelé or Ékuele, divining chain.
19. Aleyo, someone not initiated into santería.
20. Obiní, wrongly used here to mean "man." It means "woman."
21. Ifá, divining chain.
22. Oguó, money.
23. Oñí, honey.
24. Embó, charm, amulet.
25. Otí, liquor.
26. Omoyu lepe-lepe, "Watch and be quiet."
27. Epó, shea butter.
28. Emí, greeting for Changó in his avatar as drummer.
29. Cofiadeno, "Be calm."
30. Babalocha, degree of priesthood specific to men who have received certain initiations that enable them to then initiate others.
31. Obí, coconut.
32. Abure, younger sister.
33. Yemayá Saramagúa, name given to Yemayá in the prayers and songs of santería ritual.
34. Aguanillí, title given to Ogún in prayers or songs of the Yoruba ritual.
35. Moforibale, lit. "I salute you," action of greeting and showing respect to the oricha.

Part Three

1. Aura tiñosa, lit. "scabby buzzard."
2. Hato, stopping-place.
3. Sijú, nocturnal bird of prey.
4. Siguapa, small species of owl.
5. Guacamaya, wild plant with therapeutic qualities.
6. Thebaid, refers to Oedipus, king of Thebes, who went to live in a cave.
7. Brujo, lit. "sorcerer," used in times gone by to refer to practitioners of Afro-Cuban religions.

Sources

The legends, selected by Salvador Bueno, are reprinted with permission from the following sources:

Alvarado, Amérido. *7 leyendas matanceras.* Seminario *Vanguardia,* Matanzas, 1960.

Basulto de Montoya, Flora. *Cuentos y leyendas cubanas.* Compañía Editora de Libros y Folletos, La Habana, 1965.

Carbonelly y Rivero, José Manuel. *Evolución de la cultura cubana, La prosa en Cuba,* t. II. Imp. Montalvo y Cárdenas, La Habana, 1928.

Feijóo, Samuel. *Mitos y leyendas en Las Villas.* Universidad Central de Las Villas, Las Villas, 1965.

García Garófalo Mesa, Manuel. *Leyendas y tradiciones villaclareñas.* 1928.

Guirao, Ramón. *Cuentos y leyendas negras de Cuba.* Ediciones Mirador, La Habana, s/f.

Iglesia, Álvarodela. *Tradiciones cubanas.* Establecimiento Tipográfico Editorial, La Habana, 1911.

Instituto Cubano del Turismo. *Caucubú,* Colección de Tradiciones Trinitarias, Trinidad, 1954.

Instituto de Segunda Enseñanza de Camagüey. *El Camagüey legendario.* Talleres Gráficos Aral, Camagüey, 1960.

Instituto de Segunda Enseñanza de Sagua la Grande. *Folklore sagüero*, La Habana, 1940.

Lachatañeré, Rómulo. *¡Oh, Mío Yemayá!* Editorial El Arte, Manzanillo, 1938.

Martínez, Florentino. *Ayer de Santa Clara.* Universidad Central de Las Villas, Las Villas, 1959.

About the Author, Illustrator, and Translator

SALVADOR BUENO, born in 1917, is one of the foremost figures of Cuban and Latin American literary scholarship. Professor of literature at the University of Havana since 1951, he is also a founding member of the Union of Writers and Artists of Cuba (1961) and the Cuban Center of the UNESCO International Association of Literary Critics (1974). He is director of the Cuban Academy of Language, correspondent for the Royal Academy of the Spanish Language, and honorary president of the Sociedad Economica de Amigos del Pais. In the course of his extensive career as an academic, literary critic, and journalist, he has collaborated with most of the leading Cuban intellectuals of the twentieth century. He is the recipient of major awards including the Alejo Carpentier Medal and the Premio Fernando Ortiz.

Along with numerous essays and articles, some of which subsequently appeared in collected form, he has written over thirty books on literary and historical themes, many of which have been translated into other languages. These include *Medio siglo de literatura cubana, 1902–1952* [A Half-Century of Cuban Literature] (1953), *Historia de la literatura cubana* [History of Cuban Literature] (1954, 1959, 1963, 1972), *Figuras cubanas* [Cuban Figures] (1964), *Breves biografías de grandes cubanos del siglo XIX* [Brief biographies of eminent 19th-century Cubans] (1964, 1980), *Temas y personajes de la literatura cubana* [Themes and Characters from Cuban Literature] (1964), *De Merlín a Carpentier* [From Merlin to Carpentier] (1967), *Aproximaciones a la literatura hispano-americana* [Approaches to Hispano-American Literature] (1967), *Nuevas temas y personajes de la literatura cubana* [New Themes and Characters from Cuban Literature] (1977), *El negro en la novela hispanoamericana* [The Black in Latin American Literature] (1986), and *Cuba, crucero del mundo* [Cuba, Crossroads of the World] (1991). He is the editor of several anthologies, including *Antología del cuento en Cuba* [Anthology of the Short Story in Cuba] (1952), *Leyendas cubanas* [Cuban Legends] (1978), *Cuentos cubanos del siglo XIX* [Cuban Stories of the 19th Century], and *Cuentos cubanos del siglo XX* [Cuban Stories of the 20th Century] (1982).

SIEGFRIED KADEN is a painter and lecturer in fine arts. His work has been exhibited and collected by a number of major European museums, including the Munich Lenbachhaus (Museum of Contemporary Art), the Stuttgart Hospitalhof, the City of Heidelberg Museum, the Malaga Museum of Fine Arts, the Palacio de la Madraza in Granada (Spain), the Fundación Ludwig de Cuba in Havana, and the Goethe Institutes in Rotterdam and Madrid. He has held over fifty individual shows and numerous group exhibitions at major galleries and art fairs in Cuba, Spain, Switzerland, the Netherlands, and Germany. Exhibition catalogues have been published in Spain, Switzerland, Germany, and Austria. He has received numerous awards, including gold medals from the University of Vienna, the cities of Munich, Germany, and Mulhouse, Switzerland, the National Award of the State of Bavaria, and the Frankfurt International Book Fair. Specialist magazines such as *Art in America*, *ART*, and *Kunstforum International* have reviewed his work and it has been featured on public television programs in Cuba and Germany. He is the co-author and illustrator of eight books and the films, including *Hannibal* (animation, 1988), *War Games* (1995), *Little Hippology* (1996), and *Silent*

Days in Havana (1999). Currently teaching fine arts at the Escuela de Bellas Artes, San Alejandro, Havana, he has also taught at the Academy of Arts, Mannheim, the University of Weimar, and the University of Irsee in Germany, and at the Cuban Instituto Superior de las Artes Plásticas.

CHRISTINE AYORINDE, PH.D., has spent many years visiting Cuba, researching and writing on Afro-Cuban themes, religion, and questions of national identity. She is the translator of *Afro-Cuban Religions* by Miguel Barnet and *Oh, Mio Yemayá!* by Rómulo Lachatañeré. Current and forthcoming publications include chapters in *Identity in the Shadow of Slavery* and *The Yoruba Diaspora in the Americas.*